CAMBRIDGE ASSIGNMENTS IN MUSIC

Learning to Compose

JOHN HOWARD

Edited by Roy Bennett

CAMBRIDGE
UNIVERSITY PRESS

ACKNOWLEDGEMENTS

The author and publishers would like to thank the following for permission to reproduce extracts from copyright material:

pp. 22, 84 David Reck *Music of the Whole Earth*, pp. 164, 403 respectively, © 1977 David Reck, reprinted with permission of Charles Scribner's Sons, an imprint of Macmillan Publishing Company; p. 25 'America' from *West Side Story* by Leonard Bernstein and Stephen Sondheim, © 1957 (renewed) by Leonard Bernstein and Stephen Sondheim; p. 28 'Summer Night' from *An Introduction to Haiku* by Harold Henderson, © 1958 by Harold Henderson, reprinted by permission of Doubleday, a division of Bantam, Doubleday, Dell Publishing Group, Inc.; p. 47 Roy Palmer *Poverty Knock* p. 5, Cambridge University Press 1974; p. 55 Messiaen, extract from 3rd movement 'Abîme des Oiseaux' of *Quartet for the End of Time*, reproduced by permission of Editions Durand S. A., Paris/United Music Publishers Ltd; p. 56 'Boating' from *Mikrokosmos* Book V, © 1940 by Hawkes and Sons (London) Ltd, reprinted by permission of Boosey & Hawkes Music Publishers Ltd; p. 60 Charles Ives 'Charlie Rutledge', © 1920 Associated Music Publishers Inc.; p. 60 Charles Ives 'The Circus Band', reproduced by permission of Peer-Southern Organisation; p. 61 'Street Boy' by Gareth Owen from *Salford Road*, © 1974 by Gareth Owen, published by Macmillan, used by permission; p. 74 Stravinsky *The Rite of Spring*, © 1921 by Edition Russe de Musique, copyright assigned 1947 to Boosey & Hawkes Inc. for all countries, reprinted by permission of Boosey & Hawkes Music Publishers Ltd.

They would also like to thank the following for permission to reproduce photographs and other illustrative items:

pp. 6, 20, 85 (right centre) Science Photo Library; pp. 27, 31 (clock) Bridgeman Art Library; p. 28 Penny Price; pp. 31 (clouds), pp. 78, 85 (left centre) Robert Harding Picture Library; p. 43 Städtische Galerie im Lenbachhaus, München; pp. 52, 85 (top left, top right and top centre) Ardea; p. 85 (bottom centre) Jim Hansom; p. 85 (bottom right) Landscape Only.

Every effort has been made to reach copyright holders; the publishers would be glad to hear from anyone whose rights they may have unknowingly infringed.

Author's acknowledgements

I would like to thank the following for their help: Roy Bennett, Annie Cave, Chen Chi-Lin, my students, David Reck, Andy Smith and Wong Ching-Ping.

PUBLISHED BY THE PRESS SYNDICATE OF THE UNIVERSITY OF CAMBRIDGE
The Pitt Building, Trumpington Street, Cambridge, United Kingdom

CAMBRIDGE UNIVERSITY PRESS
The Edinburgh Building, Cambridge CB2 2RU, UK   http://www.cup.cam.ac.uk
40 West 20th Street, New York, NY 10011–4211, USA http://www.cup.org
10 Stamford Road, Oakleigh, Melbourne 3166, Australia
Ruiz de Alarcón 13, 28014 Madrid, Spain

First published 1990
Third printing 2000

Printed in the United Kingdom at the University Press, Cambridge

A catalogue record for this book is available from the British Library

Cover illustration by Helen Manning

ISBN 0 521 33910 3 paperback
ISBN 0 521 32599 4 cassette

NOTE TO THE TEACHER

The general approach to composition in this book is one of craftsmanship supported by listening and performance. There is no bias towards particular styles of music: style will result from individual experience and preference. Composing is both an activity and a way of thinking, encompassing all styles of music. An individual's first efforts may relate to any music; what that music may be is beyond our control, depending so much on individual experience and preference. Our work as teachers begins when we can shape people's ideas, whatever their musical affinities.

Although creativity is very important in this work, it is essential to make clear the relationship between composition and the creative area of the music curriculum. Composition is *one* way to be creative in music; there are others – for instance, in performance.

Another necessary distinction to be made is the one between composition and improvisation. They are interconnected, but composition is not a real-time activity. Composition does not have to take place within the time-framework of performing a piece of music. Improvisation, on the other hand, implies the 'real' context of musical time, within which decisions must be made instantly. Nevertheless, they can both be an individual or group activity, and group composition is very much within the philosophy of this book. Many of the assignments are equally suitable for the individual or the group, and a balanced approach to the work would probably combine both. Indeed, the assignments have been designed deliberately to cover a range of group size: it is the author's opinion that it is musically and socially desirable for pupils to make music with varying numbers of people.

The first section will enable the composer to get started, or to re-start (renew) if there is some previous experience. The succeeding sections explore the various dimensions of music by means of compositional activity. The assignments and the approach are specifically designed for the student who is working for GCSE; knowledge and experience gained earlier in the school can be built upon effectively, with the individual finding the right level at which to approach the work. Careful and sensitive guidance from the teacher is essential.

Two special features are the *Composer's resource bank* and the *Listening list*. The purpose of the *Composer's resource bank* is to act as a checklist of useful procedures in composing, and as a springboard for ideas. The *Listening list* is meant to aid teachers to devise a listening programme to support their students' composing activities.

The special cassette that accompanies this book should be a valuable support, containing sample versions of assignments as well as illustrations of techniques. The text and the cassette are carefully interlinked.

This symbol indicates recorded items on the accompanying cassette. For convenience, each item is numbered both in the book and on the cassette.

CONTENTS

AUTHOR'S **NOTE** ON THE LISTENING LIST

The *Listening list* is intended to act as a support for teaching, and is inspirational rather than prescriptive. Use made of particular pieces can be geared to the way in which pupils are developing as composers.

Section 7 of the list (Structuring) contains examples of pieces or movements which can illustrate points made in Chapter 7. Beethoven's Symphony No. 5 and the Stravinsky Symphonies of Wind Instruments are a good illustration of the structural principles of repetition, varied repetition and contrast; the Lutosławski works and the Varèse show dramatic structuring, and the Berio shows the use of language to structure music (2nd movement) and of collage and quotation (3rd movement). The other pieces are linked to Assignment 64 (p. 89) with the intention of leading pupils into more extended listening, whilst helping them to focus on structuring through the use of a simple principle. These examples have been chosen because they offer a variety of approaches in their details whilst illustrating the basic shape of an opening and a closing section, with the main body of the music in between.

GETTING STARTED

HOW TO APPROACH COMPOSING

In this book the approach to making up music is one of **craftsmanship**. You can learn a great deal from composing your own music. In fact, it is one of the most painless and stimulating ways of learning to understand how music works. The common view that composers sit around waiting for inspiration is not necessarily accurate: they work at their craft, they acquire skills and they learn from their experiences. We all have to start somewhere, and our own musical experiences are by far the best way. It is these early experiences which are most deeply embedded in our minds; we must make use of them, even as we add new experiences to them.

Two important supporting activities are **improvisation** and **listening**. You can learn a lot from making up music with other musicians, and from trying out your compositional ideas on instruments and voices. If you are happy with the music which you have composed, all well and good; if not, you will be able to make changes and immediately hear their effect. It is central to this book that you adopt this workshop style of working and also that you listen to plenty of music of a wide variety of styles. At the end of the book you will find a list of pieces recommended as a guide for your listening.

SOUNDS: THE RAW MATERIALS

If you have studied art at school, the chances are that you used a variety of different materials and techniques; also that you actually created something and that afterwards you and your teacher were able to discuss your work, to view it critically and to learn from it. This process is very much like the composition of music. It is essentially an act of making something. If you delight in making things out of sounds, in the way that you perhaps once delighted in building things out of bricks, then composition is for you. You can be captivated by it, enjoy it, and learn from it.

Here are two assignments to get you started.

Nature is full of wonderful shapes; snow-crystals for instance:

These are just examples of the rich variety of visual shapes. Nature is also full of wonderful shapes in **sound**.

Choose somewhere interesting to visit, either indoors or out: for instance, a woodland; a railway station; or inside a public library.

LISTEN for five minutes without making any sounds yourself. Afterwards, make a list of the interesting shapes in sound that you heard. Write them down in any appropriate way, showing whether they were short or long sounds, loud or soft, hard attack (beginning) or gentle attack. Here is an example.

SOUNDS MADE IN A RAILWAY STATION

Sound	short/long	loud/soft	attack
passenger sits down in train seat	quite long	soft	gentle
footsteps	short	medium to soft	hard
train door slams	short	very loud	hard
conversation	a mixture	medium	a mixture
train moving	continuous	loud	a mixture

After making your list, divide it up into human sounds, mechanical sounds and natural ones. You can now experiment with some simple drawings to represent each sound. For instance, footsteps might be drawn in this way:

This would represent somebody walking away from the listener.
The sign 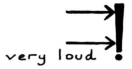 means 'getting gradually softer' (*diminuendo*).

A train door slamming might be shown like this:

Throughout your work for this assignment, remember these three stages:

LISTEN (with complete concentration)
RECALL
RECORD (in writing)

If you have portable recording equipment available, you can use this on location, listening to the recording afterwards to help you notate the sounds.

ASSIGNMENT 2 **A** Choose one instrument, for instance: a suspended cymbal (preferably a large one); a guitar; or perhaps a very simple instrument like a chime bar. Play the instrument and, as you do, thoroughly explore the sounds it can make. Experiment with loud and soft sounds, with different ways of playing the instrument (different sticks for a percussion instrument), with long and short sounds. When you have discovered a reasonable number of different sounds, write down a list of them, describing them simply.

Afterwards, examine your list and arrange the sounds into what you consider is an effective order. For instance, you might arrange them starting with the quietest and finishing with the loudest; or progressing from the lowest in pitch to the highest. Use your judgement and instinct. Then play the sounds again, this time in the order you have decided on, and, if possible, tape-record them so that you can listen to them.

Here is a summary of the different stages of this assignment:

EXPLORE on your chosen instrument

LIST the sounds

DECIDE on the order of your sounds

PLAY them

RECORD them (on tape)

LISTEN to them

B Now look again at your list and make a simple drawing beside each sound. Here are some suggestions for the cymbal.

Sound	Drawing
loud cymbal, hard stick	⌢
soft roll on cymbal	~~~~~
hit bowl of cymbal	__⌒__
a roll, getting louder then softer	⋏⋀⋁⋀⋏

Of course, these are just suggestions. You should be able to think of your own drawings.

In trying assignments 1 and 2, you have begun to compose, possibly without realising it. Your judgement has begun to be applied to sounds and the way they can be grouped and ordered. Now you can begin the next stage.

THE MUSICAL IDEA

You have begun to compose; but you may be asking yourself some questions about what you are doing. For example, how do I know whether what I make is good or not? And where does this work lead? What can I do with these musical shapes I have created? *One* answer (and it must be emphasised that it is not the only one) is to concentrate on learning how to shape something *small*, which may then be made into a passage of music or even a complete piece of music. This process can be summarised like this:

A musical idea is a very *simple* shape. It contains no padding, or obvious repetition. Here are some examples of musical ideas; you can hear them on the tape:

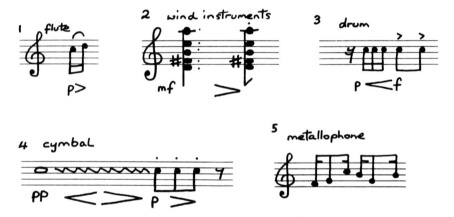

As you can see from these examples, ideas can take many different shapes. Idea 1 is a short melodic motif; idea 2 is a chord with a rhythmic outline; ideas 3 and 4 are mainly rhythmic but with the specific sound of drum and cymbal as well; idea 5 is a pattern, using rhythm and pitch.

Your musical ideas could be expressed as a tune, as a chord, as a rhythm only, or as a combination of them all. What matters most is whether or not an idea has something characteristic about it which will enable it to grow beyond itself. The keywords here are:

♦ capable of GROWTH

  and

♦ containing POTENTIAL for the future

Let us look at how we can shape our ideas.

1 As a tune

On the tape you can hear a simple melodic idea being gradually improved (or shaped). Use is made of **contour** (the pitch shape – that is, the rise and fall – of the tune), of **contrast**, and of some **unpredictability**. All three methods attempt to improve the idea so that it is better balanced.

Here is a notated version of what you have heard on the tape:

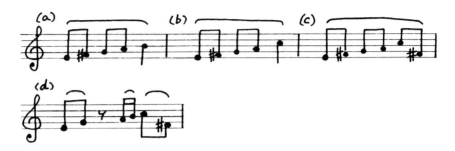

2 As a chord

You can hear a chordal idea followed through and improved on the tape.

3 As a rhythm

11

ASSIGNMENT 3 On one or several different instruments, make up a number of ideas. Listen to them and then shape each one according to the principles illustrated on the tape. When you feel reasonably satisfied with an idea, write it down in some way which seems appropriate. If ordinary staff notation fits your idea, use it; but perhaps a more graphic notation is better for your sounds. You may need to invent your own way of writing them down. In any case, try to keep your notation clear and simple.

a sliding sound

a complex sound
(e.g. lots of voices on
different notes)

short sounds, many
different notes

a sound which gets
louder and stops

gentle wave-like movement,
alternating between two notes

Remember: the sound of the music matters much more than its appearance on paper. (Nevertheless, it is a good idea to get into the habit of writing your music neatly when doing the final copy.)

Now perform your ideas to your fellow students and discuss the music with them. Swap pieces so that you can play each other's ideas.

Discuss: how well the music works

how effective the notation is

THE NEXT STAGE: HOW TO USE MUSICAL IDEAS

Let's look at this problem in a very basic way. There are three possible approaches we could adopt for making a small musical idea into a longer stretch of music:

1 By **repeating** the musical idea: this could be represented by **A** + **A** + **A**, etc.
2 By **inventing** something completely different, which either **contrasts** with the first idea or **answers** it: **A** + **B**.
3 By **varying** the first idea: (**A** + **A'** + **A"**, etc.)

On the tape, you can hear each of the above approaches illustrated, using the same basic musical idea. (Of course, it is up to the composer, in the end, to choose the approach best suited to his or her idea.) Listen to the tape and follow the notation:

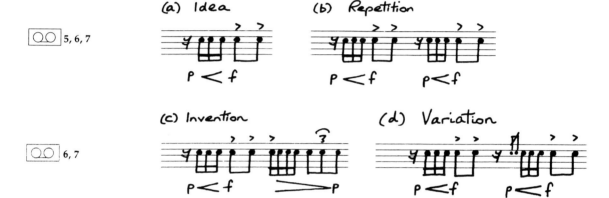

Now try the next assignment.

5, 6, 7

6, 7

ASSIGNMENT 4

Using one musical idea that you have invented, try out in turn each of the approaches shown below, so that you double (approximately) the amount of music:

- ◆ REPETITION
- ◆ CONTRAST
- ◆ VARIATION

A useful order in which to work is

COMPOSE (thinking and sketching)

NOTATE

RECORD (on tape)

Recording and playback are invaluable supporting activities for you, helping you to listen to the *effect* of what you compose: in a sense, feeding ideas back into your mind for possible adjustment or development.

When you feel that you have grasped the three approaches – and it may take several attempts – move on to the next assignment.

ASSIGNMENT 5 **A** Combine two versions of the *same* idea, played simultaneously on different instruments.

B Combine two *different* ideas, played simultaneously on different instruments. Choose two ideas which will fit together, and either have something in common, or make a satisfying contrast.

Assignments 4 and 5 contain the beginnings of two basic musical and compositional activities. Assignment 4 is the start of **melodic** thinking, although your solution does not have to be confined to melody alone. In a sense, whenever you wish to connect a sound with one which comes before or after it, you are using *melodic* thinking. Assignment 5 is the start of **harmonic** or **contrapuntal** thinking, both of which are concerned with sounds played at the same time. (You will learn more about the centrally important concept of harmony later in the book.)

Another approach to the problem of how to use a musical idea will be discovered if we look, for example, at music from Java and Bali in Indonesia. In a way, this approach is related to what we have already said about ideas. In a Javanese piece, the main source of the music is a simple tune, which all the musicians in the ensemble make use of. Usually there are twenty or more parts, all of which are related to each other: they all play more or less the same tune. This tune is known as the *balungan*, which can be translated as 'skeletal tune' (*balung* meaning 'bone' in Javanese). The tune is the skeleton of the music which must be filled out by some instruments through careful elaboration. The ensemble is known as the *gamelan*, from the word for 'hammer'; most of the instruments are percussion.

ASSIGNMENT 6 For this you need as large an ensemble as possible, with a minimum of three musicians.

(a) Study the following tune; it is the *balungan* of this piece:

(b) Divide up the group into three equal parts.
(c) Part 1 has low-pitched tuned instruments, and plays the tune very slowly.
(d) Part 2 has middle-range instruments, and plays faster, decorating the tune by filling in the gaps between the longer notes of part 1.
(e) Part 3 has high-pitched instruments, and decorates the tune with fast notes.

Work together at this, with the instruments. If you have a lot of musicians, add untuned instruments, deciding what job they can do in the music. Record the final version of the piece, then listen to it, as well as to some Javanese or Balinese music (see the *Listening list*).

 A version of this assignment is on the tape as a guide for you.

THINKING STRUCTURALLY: A BEGINNING

Most composers think in two ways at once: the first way is illustrated by what we have learnt so far: that is, the making up of musical ideas so that we can create music out of them, by expanding them. This way of thinking might be described as

◆ thinking from the inside, out

The second way of thinking is the opposite:

◆ thinking from the outside, in

Composers often move rapidly from one of these ways of thinking to the other: this helps their invention and also helps them to keep a sense of perspective about their work, rather like a painter, alternately stepping back from the canvas and working close to it.

A good word to describe this activity is **structuring** – the activity which concerns itself with the design or architecture of a piece of music.

ASSIGNMENT 7   In our work with musical ideas, we were gradually making a small idea into something larger. We are now going to make the leap from

◆ ONE sound idea

to

◆ a COMPLETE piece, approached through STRUCTURING

 Strike a large suspended cymbal *once*, quite hard, using a good-quality stick so that you get a good sound. If a cymbal is not available, use the recording of one on the tape.

Listen carefully to the sound of the cymbal, and you will notice several things about it.

1 It begins with an 'explosion' of sound.
2 It gets gradually softer over quite a long time.
3 The sound is continually changing: if you listen carefully you will hear patterns of sound, even the suggestion of a beat.
4 The initial pitch of the cymbal is actually made up of many sounds, all quite close to each other: if you play a whole armful of notes near the top of the piano, you can hear something close to this cymbal effect.
5 If you listen very carefully, you will hear some deep, quiet sounds, especially if you put your ear close to the cymbal as it gets quieter. These sounds are almost inaudible from a distance, but are very beautiful close up.

B *Draw* the sound of the cymbal, putting in as much detail as possible. For instance, the picture might look like this:

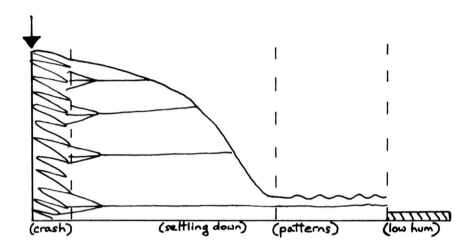

C The final stage of the assignment is to make up a piece of music for a group of instruments, *not* including the cymbal; the only 'rule' is that the complete shape or structure of your piece *must* be that of the one cymbal hit. In other words, imagine that the cymbal sound has been swollen in time, perhaps to double its length. You can use your drawing as a guide to the shape of the piece.

Make use of all the characteristics of the sound which you noticed. For instance:

- your music would begin with an explosive sound
- it would get gradually softer
- it might make use of the tiny sound patterns and beats heard on the cymbal
- it could use chords with the notes very close together

D Record your piece, and listen to it after listening again to the cymbal sound.

Binary and ternary

Two of the simplest and most effective ways of thinking structurally have been in existence for a long time. They are commonly called **binary** and **ternary**, and may be clearly expressed as **A B** (two sections of music) and **A B A** (three sections).

On the tape, you can hear an example of each. Here is the notation for you to follow:

Binary

Ternary

Although in their traditional uses, binary and ternary structures have usually been associated with tonality – the 'language' of tonic, dominant and other key relationships – they remain very useful to present-day composers of music of all kinds. This is because of their simple and natural relationship to the invention of music. They are rather like recurring shapes in nature and science.

If you make up a passage of music, you can follow it with

- ◆ something different (but not completely out of place),
  i.e. BINARY – **A B**, or
- ◆ something completely different, followed by a return of the first
  section, i.e. TERNARY – **A B A**

Both binary and ternary ways of structuring make use of **contrast**. A musical contrast can be achieved in a number of ways. Here is a list of some of them:

1 By changing the speed (tempo) of the music.
2 By making the intervals of the tune different; e.g. if there were many *leaps* in the first section, use *steps* in the second.
3 By changing the timing in some way; e.g. if there were many short notes, use longer ones. (Look at the example on page 17: in the binary version, you will see more long notes 𝅘𝅥𝅭 at the beginning of section B.)
4 By using loud and soft as a contrast.
5 By making the tune move in a different direction. (On page 17, in both the binary and ternary versions, the tune tends to move *downwards* in section A and *upwards* in section B.)

As a way of understanding this, here are two assignments in which you complete the music by making up the missing section. Don't forget that *completeness* in both binary and ternary structures depends on an effective ending to the piece.

ASSIGNMENT 8   **Binary**: add a B section to the following tune. It may be played on any suitable instrument.

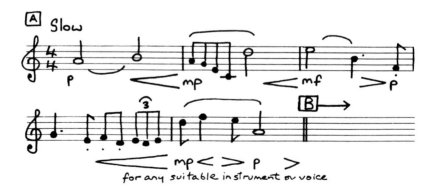

for any suitable instrument or voice

Ternary: add the middle (B) section to this tune:

Again, use any suitable instrument.

A further important thing to remember is that the return of section A in a ternary structure depends for its effectiveness on how far the middle section (B) has **travelled**: if it contains real contrast, and develops away from the music of section A, then the return of A will be all the more satisfying. Look again at the second example on page 17. In this ternary tune, at the end of section B, we have the note D. This is the highest note of the tune so far, and it is led up to by a series of steps (notes A to B to C to D). This is the climax of the tune, and we are now ready to return to section A. Section B also provides a contrast to section A. In section A, each phrase begins with high C and moves downwards in steady crotchets; in section B, each phrase begins with a dotted minim and the notes move upwards.

When you have completed assignments 8 and 9, record the whole of both tunes, then listen to them.

TEXTURE AND TIMING

These are two important parts of a composer's technique and will be developed later on in this book. Here is a brief introduction to each.

Texture

What does **texture** mean? Literally, it means the feel of the surface of cloth or other material – how the threads are organised to make the pattern. Study the different textures in cloth.

The surface of
a silk tie
(twill weave)

Twisted polyester yarns
of a textured
crêpe-de-Chine

Cotton muslin (cheesecloth)

In music, we apply the term 'texture' to sounds: the characteristic patterns into which they are arranged (woven together) during a section.

ASSIGNMENT 10

 14

Here are five descriptions of musical textures. Play the game of matching the descriptions with the five examples on the tape.

(a) Chordal, with notes close together in pitch.
(b) Four tunes at once.
(c) Chordal, with notes far apart in pitch.
(d) Short notes, isolated from each other in time.
(e) One main tune, but shared by several instruments, with others accompanying.

ASSIGNMENT 11

Compose your own versions of the above five kinds of musical texture. Perform, record and discuss them.

20

Timing

Timing can work alongside texture as an important compositional device. Here are two ways of thinking about timing:

1 How long should you make a section of music? This is important and depends on a number of things, including the position of the section in the overall structure, and whether you want it to be longer or shorter than other sections.
2 How unpredictable should the music be? It is important not to arrive at what appears to be your musical aiming point precisely at the expected moment. For instance, your tune might be moving upwards towards its highest note, and then that note is delayed by a momentary move downwards just before it. Spread things out, or compress them. Music has a psychological effect: the listener must be captivated by it. Whilst you write your music, you must act as the listener at times, hearing the music through and judging its effect in time.

ASSIGNMENT 12

Don't write anything down. Form an instrumental or vocal group with your friends. Improvise music together, playing around with (1) and (2) above. When you are pleased with a passage, record it. When you have finished, compare what you have made with what you did for assignment 2. Ask yourself how far you have travelled.

TECHNIQUES

INTRODUCTION

You have begun to compose and have explored at first hand some of the materials of composition. You have also started to consider some of the concepts that composers bear in mind when developing their craft. Now we will look in detail in chapters 1-7 at some of the essential building materials of music. These can be summarised as follows:

- ◆ TIME: beat (pulse), accent and rhythm
- ◆ TUNE: the shaping of one note after another
- ◆ CHORDS: the shaping of notes sounded at the same time
- ◆ TIMBRE: the quality ('colour') of a sound
- ◆ TEXTURE: the patterns made by sounds
- ◆ STRUCTURING: the design of music

Bear in mind that this way of looking at music is not the only way; indeed, it is the *Western* world's way. As the American composer and music educator David Reck says in his book *Music of the Whole Earth*:

We in the culture world of Western music . . . tend to look at music, all music, in a certain way. We think of it as being divided into elements like melody, rhythm, harmony, timbre, ensembles, counterpoint and polyphony, orchestrations, or form, much in the same way that medieval philosophers divided the substance of the natural world into the five elements of earth, fire, water, air, and ether. Such a way of looking at music is by no means universal . . . it is our way.

During our exploration of techniques to do with these various dimensions of music, we will be referring a great deal to non-Western music. Composing is an activity which demands a world perspective: we are interested in *all* music, whatever its origin or style.

All the building materials listed above have techniques which relate to them and which we will be considering. After we have explored **tune**, but before going on to **chords**, we will look at some aspects of the relationship between words and music. Words can sometimes be a useful building material as well.

A useful approach to acquiring techniques is to be conscious of the *effect* you want in a particular musical context, and consider technique as the means of achieving it: almost a problem-solving approach. *Don't* think in terms of needing to acquire a specific set of techniques *before* you can begin composing; to some extent, technique is personal. It needs to be acquired *through* working, rather than *before* working. Wherever we start, whatever our previous experience, we are all able to develop, or even (as this is not an area of absolute 'right and wrong') start again.

1 TIME

Time is perhaps the most important element of music; it is certainly the one which makes music so different from the visual arts. There are several ways of looking at time. It can be

◆ MEASURED
◆ constantly CHANGING
◆ CYCLIC: remembered through events which have occurred previously, and then recur
◆ PSYCHOLOGICAL and INTERNAL: in other words, time can be influenced by thoughts and feelings

All these can be reflected in music and it is exciting to consider what music each approach might produce. There are also several dimensions to musical time, all of which are valuable to the composer.

The first to consider is **pulse**, or **beat**.

PULSE or BEAT

A beat may be regular or irregular, the normal human pulse being a good example of a regular beat at a certain speed. Other less obvious examples would be

footsteps

hammering

dance steps

the wake–sleep pattern of our lives

breathing

Each of our personal heartbeats is much the same, an unending stream of impulses, but changing in speed according to the pattern of our activities. Similarly in music, beat can either remain the same or vary through acceleration and deceleration. A pulse can be drawn as follows:

• • • • • • • • • • • • • •

a pulse

ASSIGNMENT 13 1 Using a dry-sounding percussion instrument like a woodblock, try to reproduce the effect of a human pulse, making sure that you do not get faster or slower. A good trick is to count:

One and Two and Three and . . .

It is also important that each sound is equally loud. This is quite difficult to achieve, so practise it several times.

2 Now form a group of musicians and choose a conductor; perform a collective pulse, with the conductor keeping everybody together.

Instead of making each sound the same, now make a two-pattern by emphasising the 'one' of a one–two count. The conductor can help by making a downwards hand-sign on 'one', and an upwards hand-sign on 'two'.

3 Do a similar thing with the following number patterns:

three

four

five

six

Always remember to make 'one' the loudest sound, and don't get faster and faster: control the pulse.

4 Listen to Harrison Birtwistle's piece of electronic music, *Chronometer*, which explores pulse in an exciting way by making use of recordings of clocks and watches.

ASSIGNMENT 14 As an extra test of your ability to control pulse, do as follows:

1 Divide the group up equally.

2 Give each smaller group a number:

Group 1: two
Group 2: three
Group 3: four
(Don't go higher than about seven.)

3 Each group has a conductor and must clap or play their particular way of dividing the pulse. Let each group enter one by one, until there are several divisions of the same pulse going on at once. Make sure that

- everyone uses the same speed of beat
  and
- each count 'one' sounds louder than the other attacks from the group; exaggerate the difference.

You may like to introduce some kind of special sound on each count of 'one': for instance, it could be the only place at which you use a chord. Then it will stand out when each group reaches 'one'.

In much of the world's music, there is an irregularly grouped pulse: for instance, in Eastern Europe you can find pulses using mixtures of two and three like this:

24

The composer Bartók made considerable use of these kinds of grouping in his music. Listen to Nos. 2 and 4 of 'Six Dances in Bulgarian Rhythm' from *Mikrokosmos* Book VI.

In India, the use of irregular groupings can be even more complex:

and

The American composer Leonard Bernstein made interesting use of twos and threes in 'America' from *West Side Story*. The pattern there looks like this:

 15

Listen to this pattern performed on the tape. Then listen to a recording of the whole song.

ASSIGNMENT 15 1 Perform the following sequence of groups, always keeping the same speed of count:

2 Make up your own sequence of groups out of chains of twos and threes. Perform them.

We have now explored a number of important devices to do with musical time. They can be summarised as follows:

◆ PULSE or BEAT
◆ DIVISION OF A PULSE (one, two, one, two, etc.)
◆ ACCENT (each count 'one' was emphasised or accented)

In all these examples, the length of note from which the beats are constructed remains the same – a quaver: it is the distribution of the accents, separating the notes into uneven groups, that creates the effect.

ASSIGNMENT 16

Compose a piece for two percussion instruments using the following pattern for the basic beat: 2 + 3 + 2 + 2. This can be notated in quavers:

1 Make one of the instruments play the basic beat and the other one play hits or rests where you think is best, always trying to fit in with the basic 2 + 3 + 2 + 2 beat.
2 Swap over the jobs of the two instruments from time to time, so that the basic beat moves from one instrument to the other: the plan of the piece may look like this:

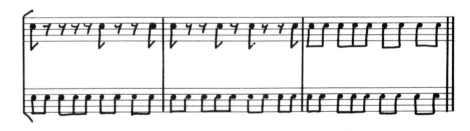

Remember: the length of each quaver count *must* stay the same. You can hear a version of this assignment on the tape.

🔘 16

ASSIGNMENT 17

Take the number 12 and experiment with methods of dividing it up into simple patterns; for instance, 2 + 3 + 2 + 2 + 3. Play your patterns; then combine with a partner, with each of you performing a different version of 12 beats at the same time.

RHYTHM

Now we will approach time from a slightly different direction and consider what rhythm is. As soon as you make even one sound, you are combining a number of elements. Your sound is at a particular frequency, or **pitch**; it has

◆ LOUDNESS
◆ COLOUR (timbre)
◆ A LENGTH OF TIME (a duration)

When associated with other sounds, it will have a particular

- ◆ PLACE in time

The last two elements work together to help create the dimension of music that we call **rhythm**.

The fundamental aspects of rhythm are

- ◆ SOUND
- ◆ SILENCE
- ◆ ACCENT/NON-ACCENT

The way in which these are associated determines the character of a rhythm: sounds group themselves into accents and non-accents (downbeats and upbeats). As part of this process, the length of each sound and each silence is of course very important, and we can usefully pursue our parallel with art:

1   You can paint a picture by covering the paper with colours and/or lines (see the example of impressionism, below).
2   Alternatively, you can use only a few brush strokes, with plenty of blank paper to help articulate the picture (see the example of Chinese calligraphy on page 42).

'Nymphéas: Pont Japonais' [Waterlilies: Japanese Bridge] by Claude Monet

The second approach is related to that of Japanese haiku poetry, which thrives on conciseness and brevity, saying a great deal in a very few words. Only three lines are used, so there is little room for detail. Here is an example in translation:

SUMMER NIGHT

A *LIGHTNING* flash:
between the forest trees
I have seen water.

from *An Introduction to Haiku* by Harold Henderson   Calligraphy by Penny Price

Neither approach is necessarily the 'right' one, but in music it is important to have a wide range of rhythmic possibilities available. Silence is not just there to be filled up; sound and silence support each other, just as lines, colours and blank space support each other in art.

ASSIGNMENT 18 **A** Improvise a piece which contains lots of different sound colours, and is crowded with sound. Do not include silence; do try to make the music as complicated in its textures as you can, for instance by having several ideas played at once. It is easier if you improvise this piece in a group of at least four: the more the better, because you will more easily achieve a crowded sound. This part of the assignment is the musical counterpart of the 'crowded' effect in impressionist painting.

Listen to 'Jeux de Vagues' from *La Mer* by Debussy, and *The Fourth of July* by Charles Ives. These two works will show you two interesting versions of this kind of texture in music.

28

B Improvise a piece which contains a large proportion of silence, using the following plan:

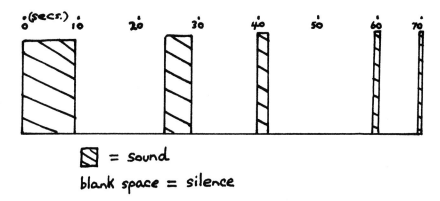

Either form a small group of about four musicians or do this individually. After each silence, try to produce sounds which are either exaggeratedly loud or soft. If you tape-record the results and listen to them, you will notice that the silences actually assist the sounds to be more effective. This is the musical counterpart of the Chinese calligraphy or the Japanese haiku poetry.

The composer Haydn was a skilled user of silence as a means of shaping music. Listen to Symphony No. 100, 'The Military', last movement. Also listen to the second of Schoenberg's *Six Little Piano Pieces*, Opus 19, which uses silence extensively.

ASSIGNMENT 19

The following four pieces use sound and silence; perform them on any instrument, and then assess the overall use of silence in each one. In the notation, a space means a silence (the longer it is, the longer the silence); a dot is a short sound.

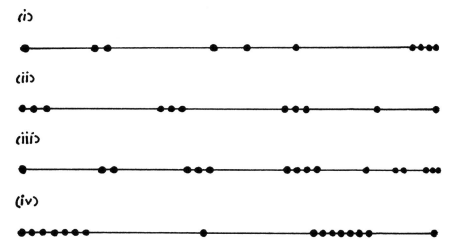

17

You can hear a performance of these pieces on the tape, but remember that each time such a piece is performed, it may be slightly different.

29

Assignments 18 and 19 have helped you to begin exploring rhythm, by playing around with time in a rather free way. Before we move on to rhythm in a more precise sense, let us consider in more detail a way of looking at time which is characteristic of composition in the 20th century, and which can also be found in music throughout the world:

- ◆ STRICT, or MEASURED TIME
- ◆ FREE, or UNMEASURED TIME

The four pieces which you have just played are from the second category: they, together with assignment 18, use a free, floating time. This notion of time behaving like a gentle stream of water characterises the music of the Japanese flute, the shakuhachi, and can also be found in

religious chant

Stockhausen's music

Indian music

A freely floating tune could be drawn like this:

ASSIGNMENT 20 1 Any combination of voices, wind and string instruments can perform this.
2 Everybody plays the same tune, as follows:

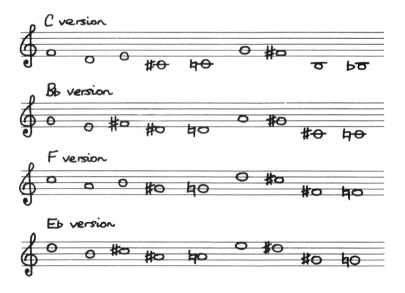

30

Clock and clouds

3 This tune, which is from my composition 'Floating' for school orchestra, should be played with each note held as long as possible: one breath per note for wind players and singers, one long bow per note for strings. Obviously, each musician moves from note to note independently.

4 Play/sing as softly as possible.

Note: the tune should sound in unison or octaves, so transposed versions for instruments like trumpet, clarinet and horn are provided.

The Hungarian composer, György Ligeti, has highlighted the two kinds of time in his imaginatively titled piece, *Clocks and Clouds*. The 'clocks' represent measured or strict time, the 'clouds' float freely.

ASSIGNMENT 21

Stage 1: Form pairs of musicians; one has a woodblock or similar dry-sounding instrument, the other a melodic instrument. Player 1 performs a pulse on the woodblock, which may vary during the piece: for instance, get faster or slower. Player 2 improvises a free-sounding melody over the pulse, using the floating kind of 'cloud' time discussed above.
Stage 2: Make a piece for two ensembles as follows:

ENSEMBLE 1: strict time
                clock-like
                dry sounds

ENSEMBLE 2: free, floating time
                cloud-like
                sonorous
                melodic

Another exciting way to approach rhythm is via words. In the music of India, a great deal of use is made of word-rhythms in the training of drummers. For instance:

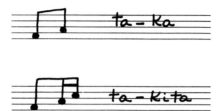

Every word has a spoken rhythm. Try speaking these out loud:

CALM

TROUBLESOME

EXCITING

LONDON

STRAVINSKY

You will have noticed that the last four words have accented syllables, and that all the words have a clear rhythmic shape. You can almost write down the rhythm of each word in musical notation:

ASSIGNMENT 22

1 Choose five words.
2 Say them aloud.
3 Write down their rhythms.
4 Compose a piece for three or more players or singers, using only the five word-rhythms. If you like, give each instrument/voice two notes only: one for accented syllables, one for the others. Or perhaps use a chord on the accents and single notes on the other syllables. Also, you could use your word-rhythms to create patterns in layers, one rhythm over the top of another until several are combined, like this:

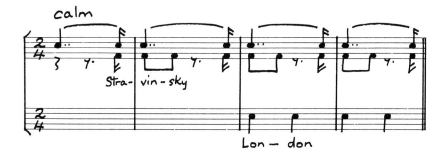

ASSIGNMENT 23   A rhythmic exercise

This exercise is designed to help rhythmic co-ordination; it is based on techniques used by Indian musicians in their training.

Study the following chart, which shows hand movements on the left, numbers of beats on the right:

a clap:	one beat
a clap and a wave:	two beats
a clap and a count on the fingers:	five beats
(The finger count is tapped out on the palm.)	

Practise each of the above. Now perform the following several times, at first slowly, then try to work faster:

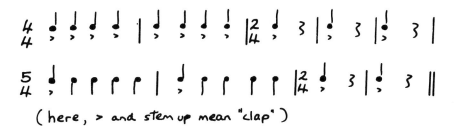

(here, > and stem up mean "clap")

Remember: all beats are of equal length. When you can perform the rhythms fluently, divide into several groups of musicians, giving each group a different sequence of the rhythmic ideas. You could even devise a way of introducing instruments and notes to this exercise – for instance, a clap could be the note C, a wave could be the note A, and so on.

In considering how to approach composing with rhythm, it is worth remembering that it does not work in isolation; it is closely associated with pitch, and particularly with contour (see the next chapter). In assignments 22 and 23 you will notice the strong influence of even a small change of pitch, from one note to another. The effect of the rhythm pattern is strengthened by the way in which pitch-changes help the accented notes.

DIVISION AND ADDITION

You will recall that we worked at methods for making musical ideas interesting in the first section of this book. What about the same thinking applied to rhythm? How can we design interesting rhythms? Of course, this is partly a 'chicken-and-egg' question. The answer depends on the character of our music in the first place – its pitch and harmonic language, its structure, and so on. But there are two ways of thinking which can help us a great deal, and which are mirrored in the work of many 20th-century composers, including Stravinsky and Messiaen. These ways of thinking are, simply,

◆ DIVISION

and

◆ ADDITION

In fact, we have already come across the idea of both division and addition when considering pulse (beat). Like so many useful musical concepts, these can be approached from different directions, according to requirements.

Division

Time can be divided up. This much is probably familiar to us, because it is exactly what a clock does for us. It may be a new way of thinking for you to imagine that rhythms are being created by dividing up time. Think of a long note value, say a semibreve. The following chart shows how, first, simple rhythms can be made out of it, and then gradually more complex ones.

 18

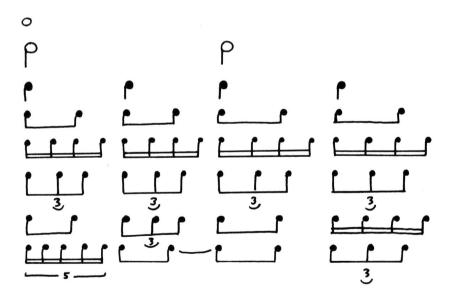

On the tape you can hear this process followed through from semibreve to complex rhythm.

Western music, in fact, tends to divide the spaces between beats into either 2 or 3, so that we have:

8		12
4	or	6
2		3
1		1

Sometimes, as we have seen in relation to pulse, we have *combinations* of 2 and 3.

In non-Western music, however, other divisions are used, commonly:

5　　7　　9

These divisions have become much more common in 20th-century Western music, and can be notated like this:

If you need an easy way of imagining how a beat can divide into 5 and 7, try saying

LOLLOBRIGIDA (= 5)

GINA LOLLOBRIGIDA (= 7)

(Of course, all syllables must be given equal length to make this work.)

ASSIGNMENT 24　　Compose a rhythmic study for three instruments, giving each one a complete repertoire of rhythms made out of a long note. Use both 2 and 3 to divide the note, and 5 and 7. For instance:

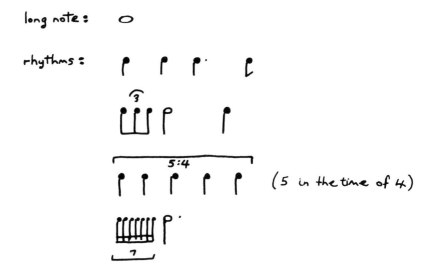

You can hear an example of a rhythmic study on the tape; here is its notation:

Addition

Addition is also an interesting way of creating rhythms. For instance, look at what happens if you make the following sequence of numbers into musical note-lengths:

2 + 3 + 5 + 2 + 3 + 3 + 3 + 2 + 6 + 5 + 2 + 2

Of course, this assumes that we are keeping the same length of beat all the time. But what will result if we add together note-lengths calculated by using *different* beat lengths?

You will notice that the length of beat alters with nearly every note, starting with a quaver beat, then a crotchet beat, back to quavers, and so on. (The beat length is sketched above the notes of the rhythm.)

The work which probably did most to alter the 20th century's way of dealing with musical time is Stravinsky's *The Rite of Spring*. Here rhythm and the measurement of time (metre) are central, and the additive principle underpins everything. Here are two examples of this from *The Rite of Spring*:

ASSIGNMENT 25

Compose four different rhythms, each with a different time-signature. Make them each about three bars long. Use a crotchet beat for the first and third rhythms, a quaver beat for the second and fourth. Now experiment with the rhythms as follows:

1 Play them through, without leaving a break between each one and the next. In other words, make a continuous line out of them.
2 Cross off one bar from each rhythm. Experiment with them to find the most appropriate order. In the version below and on the tape, the $\frac{3}{4}$ and $\frac{5}{8}$ rhythms changed places as the music developed because this seemed the best order.
3 Cross off another bar from each. Play.
4 Add notes to the rhythm you ended up with in (3). Play it through.
5 So far, you should have kept the same tempo for each rhythmic 'block'. In other words, a quaver remains the same length. Finally, experiment with sudden changes of tempo from one 'block' to another. For instance, try making the crotchet of blocks (1) and (3) equal in length to *three quavers* in blocks (2) and (4). Assess the different effect created by this change.

On the tape, you can hear a version of this assignment. Its notation looks like this:

Peter Maxwell Davies's piece *Antechrist* contains many interesting and complex metrical relationships and it will be interesting for you to listen to it and follow the score as an extension to the work you have just been doing.

DECORATION OF A BEAT

Another approach to musical time is to consider what happens if you take a basic beat and **decorate** it. This can be done in three ways:

1 By playing just before the beat.
2 By playing just after the beat.
3 By dividing up the beat equally.

The third one of these we have already explored in looking at division. Experiment in pairs with the first two: one musician plays the main beat, the other plays just after or before it. Then try the next assignment.

ASSIGNMENT 26

Version A

Instrument 1: plays a tune, in free time.
Instrument 2: plays a repeating accompaniment pattern, in strict time; for example:

Version B

Instrumental group 1: plays the tune, mainly in unison, but with decoration.
Instrumental group 2: plays an accompaniment pattern with a main beat, which is decorated by some instruments playing just before or after the beat.

21 There is a version of this assignment on the tape.

The approach to musical time using division finds one of its most sophisticated expressions in the music of Bali and Java, where musicians play music that is organised very carefully around a main tune. (You will find further ideas from Bali on page 14.) The method can be depicted, in a simplified way, like this:

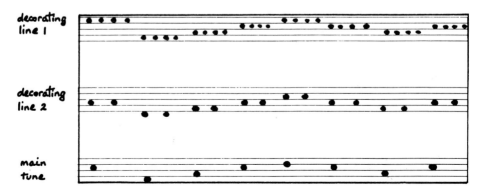

We have discussed numbers a great deal in relation to time. Division and addition are useful; you may like to consider where multiplication fits into this. If we take a basic rhythmic shape and multiply it, what we are doing is to create the beginnings of a musical structure. For example:

Later we will be returning to structural thinking. In the meantime, this notion of multiplication may help you to see how small ideas and large ones can be related.

In thinking about musical time, it is a very good thing to sort out in your mind what some of the words mean which musicians frequently use. Here is a list of some of the ones that we have considered; spend some time exploring their meaning, and thinking about how they may fit into your music:

◆ METRE
◆ RHYTHM
◆ ACCENT/NON-ACCENT
◆ UPBEAT/ DOWNBEAT

2 TUNE

LINE AND CONTOUR

The idea of melody (tune-making) is probably one of the first things we think about when trying to imagine music. It is entirely within everybody's ability to create or re-create a tune in the mind, although sometimes a little training is needed to make people appreciate their own ability. This imaginative skill goes a long way towards helping us to compose our own melodic lines, but we also need a number of techniques in order to shape what we have imagined. For instance, we can learn to give a line a sense of

◆ BALANCE

This is an easy notion to grasp, if you imagine your whole line as though it were a visual thing: a piece of architecture or sculpture. If the melodic line explores a certain pitch range, then ask yourself if it does so in a *balanced* way. What is balance? How do we know we have achieved the *right* balance? Do we return to the lowest point, or is it used only at, say, the start? Do we have a reasonably large pitch area, or are we confined? Interestingly, different parts of the world have different attitudes to balance in tune-making. We might say that balance implies a balanced coverage, over a period of time, of the pitch range used by a tune: balanced, but not too predictable.

Study the following melodic lines and ask these questions and others about the balance of the line:

ASSIGNMENT 27   Now take the following beginnings and complete the melodic line in each case; they are all for the voice, so sing your complete version of each one when it is completed; then compare versions that your friends have made with yours:

 23

You can hear the beginnings on the tape.

Having thought about balance, we should also explore

◆ CONTOUR

In this respect, if we are thinking of our melodic lines in a visual way, the art of drawing can help us a great deal. On the next two pages are two interesting examples of lines, one from Chinese calligraphy and the other from the artist Paul Klee. These repay careful study, and then translation into music, because they offer a rich and varied attitude to contour.

ASSIGNMENT 28

 24

Choose one of the illustrations on the next two pages. Create a musical version of it, played/sung by one instrument/voice. There is a version of the Chinese figure (which means 'a thousand') on the tape.

Remember:

1 Up and down on the drawing = up and down in pitch.
2 Across = time.
3 A line in the drawing may not show every note of the equivalent musical line, just the general directions; you can use subtle changes of direction in the notes of your tune which are not indicated in the drawing.

There are two important techniques with regard to contour: one is to create a contour by taking long notes and filling in the space between them in as interesting a way as possible. Here is an example of this, which can also be heard on the tape:

 25

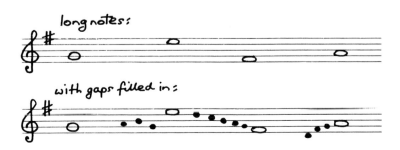

41

The Chinese ideogram for 'a thousand'

The second technique is to do with direction. Obviously music cannot always move in one pitch direction all the time; one way of making pitch contour interesting is to make its direction unpredictable by using a mixture of steps and leaps. (You will probably have begun to do this in assignment 28.) Here is an example:

'Erzengel' [Archangel] by Paul Klee

ASSIGNMENT 29 Out of the long notes illustrated below, construct an interesting line by filling in the gaps; use a carefully judged combination of steps and leaps. Play the line on a suitable instrument.

ASSIGNMENT 30 Using the line made up in the previous assignment, add exact note lengths to make the music even more interesting. Remember: contour works hand-in-hand with time in creating effective music, and i⁺ partly depends on how quickly or slowly you move through part of a line whether it works or not.

Study these examples of excellent musical lines, from music by Bach, Beethoven and Handel, and see if there are common methods employed. Measure them against each of the techniques we have learnt:

- ◆ pitch balance
- ◆ contour: direction (unpredictability)
- ◆ contour: relation to time

Bach, 'The 48', Book 1

Beethoven, Sonata, Op. 79

Handel, Courante from Suite in G

Now let's approach the same issue, that of contour, from a different direction. In the above ideas, we began by being disciplined, gradually building up a picture of a good musical line. The following assignment encourages a freer attitude to melody.

ASSIGNMENT 31

Compose a tune for the voice, containing three sections as follows:

Section 1: very wide intervals between notes

Section 2: very narrow intervals

Section 3: a mixture of the two

Record yourself, singing your tune.

Before leaving the idea of contour, consider some of the ways of creating it that are found in the world's music. At the top of the next page is a brief list of possible approaches. Beside each one you can see both a drawing of its shape, and its possible musical notation.

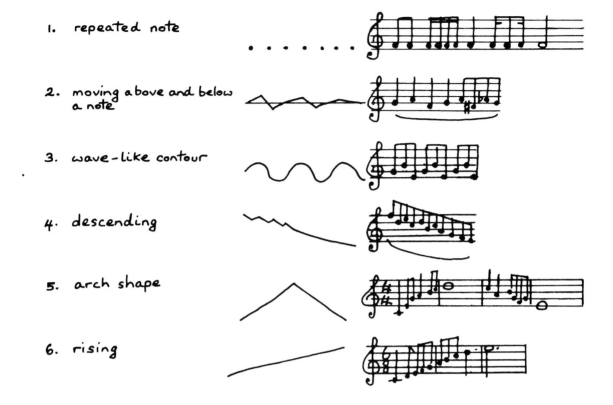

1. repeated note

2. moving above and below a note

3. wave-like contour

4. descending

5. arch shape

6. rising

ASSIGNMENT 32

27

On any instrument or voice, compose a version of each of the above contours. If you like, do each one for a different instrument. An example of each shape is given on the tape.

In our study of line and contour, we must remember that, as in all aspects of composition, there are no rules as such. Decisions have to be made, and followed through in a consistent manner. Yet different cultures have different views of what constitutes an effective melodic line. Study the following five examples – and discover some of your own:

(a) Bali   (intervals are approximate here)

(b) N. American Indian

(c) India

(d) China

(e) N. American Indian

PHRASING

We have yet to discuss one of the most important aspects of musical line: the notion of phrasing. The best way of beginning to understand what this means is to think of it in relation to breathing. A singer or a player of a wind instrument is forced to breathe, and usually looks for the end of a phrase in order to do it. In other words, what a phrase is, and its length, are closely connected with the human breathing span. It is interesting to note that this aspect of our own physiology affects even the music of instruments which do not need breath – the piano, for instance.

Another way of understanding phrasing is to think of it as a way of making sense of a long stretch of music – of taking it in in manageable bits, as it were.

ASSIGNMENT 33

Pair up with another musician; each player has one melodic instrument. Improvise as follows:

Player 1: a phrase

Player 2: an answering phrase

Player 1: a second phrase

Player 2: another answer

Continue in this way, gradually building up a musical conversation. (You can hear an example of a conversation between two instruments on the tape.)

This assignment should be attempted again and again, so that both players come to understand the nature of a questioning phrase, and that of an answering one.

Now listen to some music which contains interesting use of this conversational principle. There are many examples in the work of the jazz musicians Miles Davis and Charles Mingus, and the Classical masters of the art of balanced phrasing were Mozart and Haydn. Listen to the slow movement of Mozart's Clarinet Quintet, and Mingus's piece *Mariachis* (*The Street Musicians*).

What is becoming apparent here is that there is a strong parallel relationship between music and language. For instance, if you read aloud, you will soon come to appreciate the way in which a text is divided up into phrases, sentences, paragraphs, and so on. You will also feel the sense of rise and fall which a line of words can possess. We call the falling aspect of this the cadence – and as you will probably know, there is a musical parallel here, in that music has a sense of cadence as well.

ASSIGNMENT 34

Part 1

Either select a passage from a book or newspaper, or use the following text:

Primitive work processes were often accompanied by singing. Spinning and weaving, for example, or soothing a baby to sleep, or milking a cow, had songs with rhythms appropriate to the activity concerned. Apart from such individual tasks, team work was often accompanied by song. The sea shanties of the last century are group work songs as are the chants of the Hebridean cloth fullers and the Portland quarrymen, which survived until very recent years.

In addition to these work songs, people frequently made songs about work. These might be descriptions of various crafts and trades, sometimes highly romanticised, and often full of jaunty good humour.

from *Poverty Knock* by Roy Palmer

Read this passage aloud, appreciating the organisation of the text into phrases, sentences and paragraphs. Note carefully the length in time of each section, so that you have an idea of the structure of the whole text.

Now create a musical counterpart to the text, for solo instrument; of course, you will not be able to use any of the actual words, but you should use everything else about the text, such as the lengths of phrases and sentences, and the pitch contour of them. The phrase 'soothing a baby to sleep' from the above text has a contour which could be drawn as follows:

The musical counterpart of this might be the following clarinet line, which you can hear on the tape:

○○ 29

If, instead, you choose a dramatic passage with an identifiable climax, so much the better – you will be able to mirror that in your music.

Part 2

Use the same text, but this time create a piece of music using the vocal (word) sounds of the text only: no instruments or conventional singing allowed. Think of the text as your material – to be made more and more like a piece of music, until it *is* music.

In attempting Part 2, you may achieve better results with a *group* of people; then you can experiment with 'orchestration' of the text:

solos (single voices)

duets (two voices)

tuttis (many voices together)

Now combine Parts 1 and 2 into one performance, perhaps simultaneously, or arranged in some appropriate way.

FINDING NOTES FOR TUNES: SCALES

Scales are a convenient way of demonstrating the set of notes in use in a piece or pieces. Looked at from another point of view, they are also a useful resource for tune-making. Just as we can invent tunes by filling in the gaps between long notes, so we can invent by

◆ omitting some of the notes from a scale

◆ using any patterns of notes that the scale suggests

For instance, the following scale of notes

can produce this simple tune:

Remembering that our Western scales only represent a small part of music, and that scales result from music, not the other way round, we should try inventing from a few different scales.

Investigate the following three scales. Invent a tune for a suitable instrument or voice from each of them.

It is interesting to use the scale to define the range of a tune: in other words, the highest note of the scale will be the highest note of the tune. You may also consider whether all the notes in each of the above scales are of equal importance, or whether some are better for ending on than others.

FINDING NOTES FOR TUNES: CHORDS

Chords can also act as a resource in inventing the notes of a tune. The music of Haydn and Mozart is full of tunes created out of chords. For instance, study these tunes from Mozart:

The brackets show where notes have been invented out of chords. These tunes use chords which are commonplace and easily formed. We can also use more complex chords – for instance, these three chords

can generate these tunes:

ASSIGNMENT 36

1 From the above three chords, create two tunes for any instrument.
2 Accompany the tune with the three chords, played in the correct order, on another instrument or instruments.

DEVELOPING A TUNE

These three ideas for making more out of a tune will remind you of those which we explored at the beginning of the book: repetition, invention and variation (see page 13). When extending our tunes, we don't have to keep creating new material; rather, we can help our composing by using the following techniques for creating more out of what we already have.

By variation

This principle can be used in two ways.

The first of these takes a small melodic cell or group of notes, and repeats it with tiny changes as the music proceeds. The following cell

could produce these variations of itself:

 30

You can hear this cell and its variations on the tape. Such an approach is common in African music.

The second use of variation produces greater contrast; this is when we take a group of notes – this, for instance –

and move, or transpose, the whole group so that it starts on a higher or lower note. The shape, of course, remains much the same. Here are two examples of this at work; you can hear them on the tape and should be aware of the change which occurs when we transpose (literally, change the position of) a group of notes:

(a)

 31

(b)

By organic growth

Imagine a tiny melodic idea, for instance:

Now think of this idea gradually growing, like a plant or a tree:

This kind of melodic growth may be found frequently in European classical music: for instance, in the first movement of Beethoven's Symphony No. 5 in C minor. It can also be found in the melodies of Japanese music.

Pasque flower
(*Anemone pulsatilla*)

ASSIGNMENT 37

1 **Improvise** on the following idea; try to create out of it a tune which grows.

2 Using the same idea, **compose** a tune which grows out of it. Ask a fellow musician to record it for you on any suitable melodic instrument.

By decoration

There are many ways of decorating a tune. Compare a tune with virtually no decoration, like this chorale

52

with this, a piece for the Chinese ch'in (a kind of zither) which contains many
different kinds of decoration (or ornament):

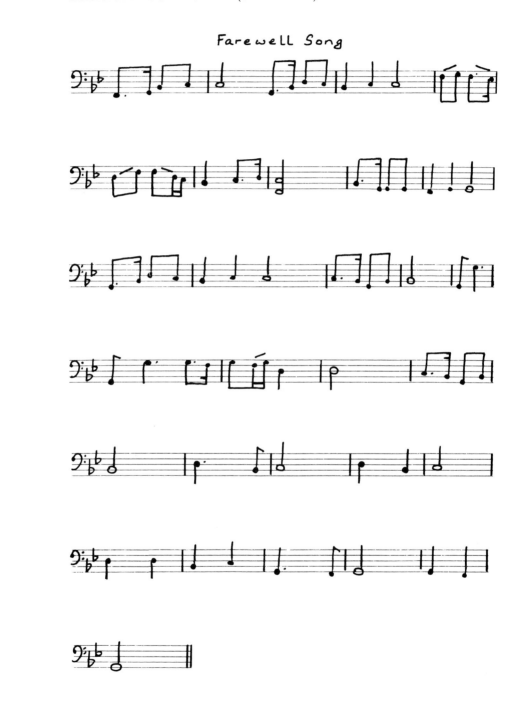

Farewell Song

32

In our work with contour, we learnt the technique of filling in other notes
between the main notes of a tune. This use of 'unessential notes' is a
common way of decorating a tune. The unessential notes are often the ones

which are *not* created out of chords. In Western music, we frequently also use the following to decorate a musical line:

◆ the trill (rapid alternation of two notes)

◆ the leaning note (appoggiatura)

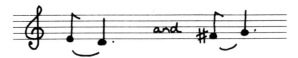

◆ 'free' or 'grace' notes,
as single notes:

or as groups:

The following tune for clarinet makes use of all these. Study it and listen to it on the tape.

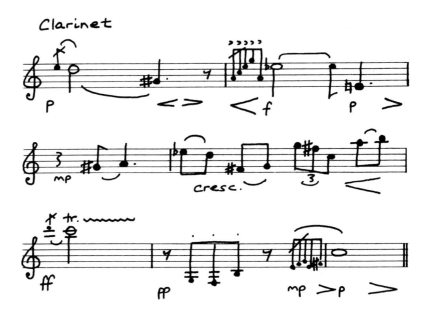

ASSIGNMENT 38 **A** Listen to the clarinet solo (the third movement, 'Abîme des Oiseaux') from Messiaen's *Quartet for the End of Time*. Here is part of it:

Note: Photocopying of the above music is illegal.

B Add decorations to the following lines for clarinet:

TUNE + ACCOMPANIMENT

Although we can do a great deal of valuable work with melody alone, most tunes are accompanied by something. These accompaniments can be very sophisticated, as in the songs of Schubert. Listen, for example, to *Erlkönig* (The Erlking).

On the other hand, there are a number of simple types of setting for tunes which we can use quite easily.

The first of these is to add a **drone**, or continuous note, to the tune. This is found in bagpipe music, for instance. The drone can also become more than one note: commonly two notes a bare fifth apart.

ASSIGNMENT 39 Experiment with adding to a tune

a drone note

a fifth (two-note) drone

a complete chord

We can also add an **ostinato** pattern to a tune. Ostinato means 'obstinately the same' and is used to refer to a pattern of pitch and/or rhythm which stays the same. Here is an example of this kind of setting for a tune, from a piece by Bartók called 'Boating' (*Mikrokosmos* Book V):

Allegretto

This is the ostinato being used:

ASSIGNMENT 40

1 Make up a pattern for use as an ostinato. Play it on one instrument, while your fellow musician improvises a tune to go with it. Now swap over, so that you improvise.
2 Write a tune for keyboard to be played by the right hand. Add to it a left-hand ostinato.

◯◯ **34**   You can hear a version of this assignment on the tape.

(You will find a brief summary of tune-making techniques in *A composer's resource bank* at the end of the book.)

3 WORDS

Here we are concerned with the aspect of words which follows on naturally from our consideration of rhythm, line and contour. To anyone who wishes to compose for the voice, words are of obvious importance and present us with a range of exciting possibilities.

The composer has four important things to consider when setting words:

1 The actual choice of text.
2 The way in which that text should be set to music, bearing in mind that, however great the poetry, the music must be able to add an extra dimension to it – otherwise the music is not really needed at all.
3 The suitability of the text for the voice.
4 The likely conflict between words and music. To borrow the title of R. Murray Schafer's book, *When Words Sing*, you have to consider whether to have:

> one note per syllable (= clearly understandable words)
> or
> a curve of notes on a syllable (= effective music).

Of course, often the answer lies in a combination of the two.

Let us consider the choice of text first. It is sensible to avoid setting one of the acknowledged poetic masterpieces, partly because such works are very well known, and partly because music probably has nothing to add to the artistic quality of such works.

The choice must to some extent be a personal one: the words must fire your imagination so that your music will possess a life of its own. For this reason, it may well be a good idea to collaborate with somebody you know, and ask them to make up the words, because this may produce a more interesting result. You may like to make up your own words. (The composer Michael Tippett wrote both the words and the music for his oratorio *A Child of Our Time*.)

What about the actual setting of the words? First you must get to know the sound of the text very well by reading it aloud. Then look for the metre – the pattern of accent and non-accent. Putting it simply, the main accented notes of the music must coincide with the accented syllables in the words.

ASSIGNMENT 41 **A** Choose three short poems: nursery rhymes would do well. Make a study of the accent patterns of each one, marking above the syllables whether they are accented or not; the signs

He thought he saw a Rattlesnake

are often used for this in the study of poetry.

Here is an example of a suitable text:

He thought he saw a Rattlesnake
That questioned him in Greek,
He looked again and found it was
The Middle of Next Week.
'The one thing I regret,' he said,
'Is that it cannot speak!'
　　(from *Sylvie and Bruno* by Lewis Carroll)

B Compose a tune for one of the texts, and either sing it yourself or get someone to do it for you. Listen for the way words and music fit.

Suitability of the text for singing is an area of judgement which improves with experience. Nevertheless, there are some guidelines which can help.

First, suitability depends on the way you choose to set the text to music. If you place a difficult syllable on a high note, then you will cause awkwardness; high notes need easy, open vowels.

Secondly, if you have a succession of hard consonants, then make the rhythm suitably strong.

Thirdly, avoid making unimportant words sound important: look for the special words on which you can do something extra.

Fourthly, suitability also depends on the type of language used. Ask yourself what is the style of this poetry: is it high-flown and romantic, or colloquial and everyday-sounding? Matching the poetic style may be a good reason for adjusting the nature of your music.

Here, some study of the marriage of words and music in reggae would certainly repay you. Reggae songs, for instance those of Bob Marley, are a rich source, demonstrating a near-perfect blend of poetic and musical styles. Listen to the examples of Marley's work, 'Chant Down Babylon' and 'Buffalo Soldier', which are both on his LP *Confrontation*.

One last thing about word-setting: it can be useful to use a device known as **word-painting**. This means actually trying to 'paint' a word from the text in the music in a simple way. It could be as simple as making the music go up in pitch because the text talks of going up; or using a particularly 'biting' chord on the word 'cold'.

The madrigal composers of 16th-century England delighted in the use of this technique; for instance, listen to 'As Vesta was from Latmos Hill descending' by Thomas Weelkes. The interesting uses of word-painting occur at

'running down'

'two by two'

'three by three together'

'all alone'

Weelkes's 'O Care, thou wilt despatch me' is another good madrigal in which to listen for special settings of words. See what you can discover in it for yourself. The words of the first part are printed on the next page.

O Care, thou wilt despatch me,
If music do not match thee.
                Fa la la.
So deadly thou dost sting me,
Mirth only help can bring me.
                Fa la la.

You can find more modern examples in the music of Britten and Tippett. Listen to the 'Nocturne' and 'Hymn' from Britten's *Serenade* for tenor, horn and strings (also a good work to study for word-setting in general) and Tippett's *A Child of Our Time*. Listen to the opening chorus of this work: 'The world *turns* on its *dark* side'. Each of the words 'turns' and 'dark' is portrayed in a particularly striking way in the music.

There are interesting, and occasionally bizarre, uses of this technique in the music of the American composer, Charles Ives. Investigate his songs 'The Circus Band' and 'Charlie Rutledge'.

'The Circus Band'

(a)   Ives makes the music 'prance' at the words 'horses are prancing':

(b)   at 'Where is the lady all in pink' Ives imitates circus band trombones on the piano.

'Charlie Rutledge'

(a)   heavy piano chords at:
'a man both tough'

(b)   when Charlie's horse gets faster, so does the music (accelerando)

Such methods can be fun to use and to identify, and in a very straightforward way help to connect words and music. Of course, they do depend on the composer's view of how to reflect a word in the music.

Set the following text to music:

> *Street Boy*
>
> *Just you look at me, man*
> *Stompin' down the street*
> *My crombie's stuffed with biceps*
> *My boots is filled with feet.*
>
> *Just you hark to me, man*
> *When they call us out*
> *My head is full of silence*
> *My mouth is full of shout.*
>
> *Just you watch me move, man*
> *Steady like a clock*
> *My heart is spaced on blue beat*
> *My soul is stoned on rock.*
>
> *Just you read my name, man*
> *Writ for all to see*
> *The walls is red with stories*
> *The streets is filled with me.*
>
> (by Gareth Owen, from *Salford Road*)

In your music, try to paint the following words from the text:

Stompin'

clock

rock

4 CHORDS

There is a great deal of mystique surrounding the area of music known as **harmony**. Harmony is what happens when two or more notes are sounded at once (a chord), and this is followed by another chord, making a progression. The myth is that you have to work according to a rule book, and that only certain sounds fit with other sounds. Without dwelling upon the complexities of this area (this book does not set out to be a textbook on 'traditional' harmony), we will explore here two parallel approaches to harmony. At the same time, it is essential to emphasise the value of **experiment** with regard to chords. Try out different combinations of sounds, and when you find something you like, save it in some way, perhaps by recording it, storing it in an electronic keyboard, or simply writing it down in a sketchbook. You can then use a chord or a combination of chords whenever it becomes appropriate – which could be some time later.

The first approach is very useful in both improvisation and composition, and uses the three most important chords within a key.

These are

◆ TONIC

◆ DOMINANT

and

◆ SUB-DOMINANT

These are built up on the first, fifth and fourth notes of the scale, and each uses the same interval shape. Working from the bottom note up, they are formed by

going up a major third (= four semitones)

from the middle note, going up a minor third (= three semitones)

In the key of C major these chords look like this:

For convenience, we often know these chords by the number which identifies their main note, or **root**. The root is often – but not always – the lowest note of the chord. This means that:

◆ TONIC chord   = I

◆ DOMINANT chord   = V

◆ SUB-DOMINANT chord = IV

Find an instrument that will play chords; or form a group with enough players to share out the notes of a chord between melodic instruments (a minimum of three). Work out the notes of chords I, IV and V in turn.

1 Play the chords in the order I, IV, V, and keep repeating the cycle of three chords.
2 Add another player, and ask him or her to make up a tune above the chords.

Swap over, so that each player has a turn at being the melodic improviser. You can hear a version of this assignment on the tape.

⚟ 35

The purpose of this work is to get the feeling for these three basic chords 'into your blood'. Now it can be very useful to you. You can compose with these chords, for instance playing around with the order in which they are used, perhaps adding other notes to them, to see (hear) what effect is produced. If you have even the simplest electronic keyboard, you can use its automatic chord facility, which is usually based on a selection of simple chords including I, IV and V. If you play:

C   F   G

in the lowest register of the keyboard with the chord facility switched on, you will get chords I, IV and V.

It cannot be emphasised too strongly that improvising and composing with these three chords will pay dividends for you later, giving you the foundations of a harmonic sense which is valuable whatever your chosen musical style.

In a sense, this assignment is a more sophisticated version of the previous one. This time, you are given a 'blues' chord sequence on which to improvise. Again, you can make this a solo or a group exercise, with a group sharing out the notes of the chords. The chord pattern is

I⁷ IV⁷ I⁷ V⁷ IV⁷ I⁷

The figure [7] means that we are adding a fourth note to each chord, seven notes above the root. In C major, the chords will look like this:

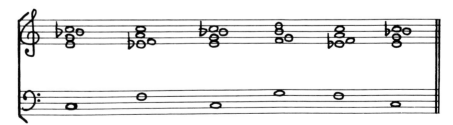

A convenient and stylistic way of organising the time is to base the music in 4, with each chord being played four times to make up a whole bar. This

63

timing fits the style of blues. Notated, it looks like this:

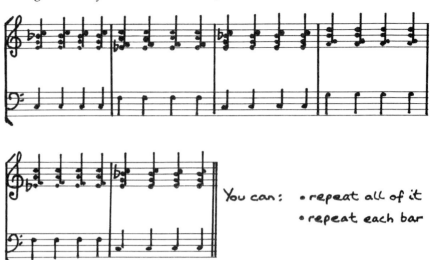

You can: • repeat all of it
         • repeat each bar

🔾🔾 36 and you can hear this chord sequence on the tape.

When you have worked out the chord pattern, take it in turns to improvise solos above it. Work at this regularly, perhaps ten minutes at the beginning of each lesson for a term, and you will become confident blues improvisers, and you will also enjoy yourselves.

ASSIGNMENT 45 Another way of working with chords I, IV and V is to harmonise a well-known tune using them; for instance, one like 'When the Saints'. Make an arrangement of such a tune (your teacher will help you choose a suitable one) by working through the following stages:

1 Harmonise the tune by adding the three chords in appropriate places.
2 Make up an accompanying rhythmic pattern.
3 Give the tune to one instrument, the chords to another, the bass line to another and allocate the rhythm to drums or other percussion. Record the instrumental group performing your arrangement.

Our second approach to harmony is completely different. If music is not within the major–minor key system, then it needs to use other principles to organise its harmony. One of these is to use the interval (the pitch space between two notes) as a way of creating chords. For instance, a chord could be created using very few types of interval between its notes, or even just one type. Here is an example of a chord made out of seconds (pairs of neighbouring notes):

and here is a characteristic chord made out of fourths:

 38

On the other hand, you might create a chord using many types of interval. Here is an example:

 39

The main thing to avoid in this kind of harmony is the *obvious* use of the octave between notes. Here is an example of too obvious an octave relationship:

 40

The next example is much better, because the octave between G and G' has been disguised:

 41

ASSIGNMENT 46   Compose a pattern of six different chords, each one organised through its intervals. Orchestrate your chords for whatever group of players is available – the school orchestra or band perhaps – and then perform and record them. You could experiment with the order in which the chords are played.

You may like to take this further, and compose a complete piece out of your chord-pattern, perhaps adding tunes to go with it.

5 TIMBRE

One of most important building-blocks in music is something known as the **harmonic series**. This is a natural sequence of notes, which always has the same interval pattern, and applies to every sound made out of regular vibrations of the air. That includes all conventional musical notes. The main, lowest note of the series is known as the **fundamental**. Above the fundamental, the higher notes, or **harmonics**, form the following interval pattern. (The notes marked * are not in tune with any normal scale in use.)

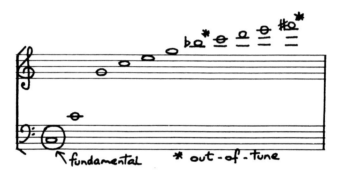

In fact, this is only part of the series, because it continues, getting higher and higher, until human ears are unable to hear any more harmonics.

Hearing harmonics

ASSIGNMENT 47

1 Use any brass instrument. Play up from the lowest 'open' note, without using valves (or, in the case of the trombone, the slide), but using lip pressure only to obtain the different pitches. This provides a good aural demonstration of the sound of part of the series. You should be able to hear the following sounds at least:

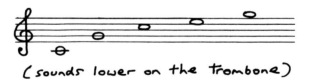

2 On the piano, hold down, without actually *sounding* them, the following notes:

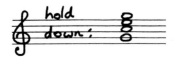

Strike this note

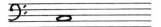

as loudly as possible and

LISTEN.

You should hear some of the harmonics which sound above the note C.

ASSIGNMENT 48 Compose a short study using

1 the open notes of a brass instrument;
2 the way of producing harmonics on the piano which we have just tried out.

 42 There is a version of this assignment on the tape.

TWO IMPORTANT CHARACTERISTICS OF THE HARMONIC SERIES

1 The notes get closer to each other the higher you go up the series.
2 Harmonics are present in the sound of an instrument, and it is their particular combination which helps to make one type of instrument sound different from another. In other words, an instrument will have some harmonics which are strongly present in its sound, and some which are weak; another instrument will have a different arrangement of strong and weak. This is rather like having a musical fingerprint.

WHAT IS TIMBRE?

The word really means

◆ COLOUR of sound

The colour of a sound is made up of several elements:

1 Its particular combination of **harmonics**.
2 The **shape** of the note sounded. This is called the **envelope** of a sound, meaning its use of three elements:

◆ ATTACK (beginning)
◆ SUSTAIN (middle)
◆ RELEASE (end)

Study these three drawings of different envelope patterns:

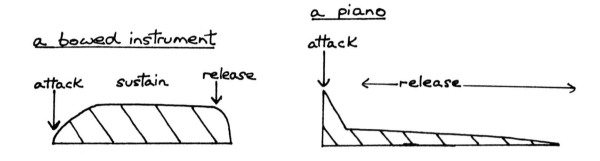

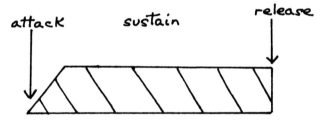

In itself, envelope is a useful characteristic of sound. It can even help us create the structure of a piece out of the characteristics of one sound (see chapter 7).

3 The **resonance** of the sound. This refers to the way in which the materials from which the instrument is constructed influence the sound, and the way in which the air within the instrument is allowed to vibrate. Compare:

a violin

with an oboe

with a Chinese p'i-p'a

In your composing, you need to make timbre work for you. It can be a very exciting dimension of music, especially if you apply all that we have just said to *combinations* of instruments/voices as well as to individual ones.

ASSIGNMENT 49 A Collect, draw and record four sounds with *different* envelopes. Draw their envelopes, using the examples opposite as models. Make a short piece out of the contrast between them.

B Choose four instruments that can all play the same pitched note. Experiment with different combinations of them on that note. Make a short piece, exploring the different timbres you can create on that one note.

ASSIGNMENT 50 Collect fifteen different timbres. Record them and make a list, describing them in as much detail as possible. As a guide, here are some ideas:

a nasal voice

a drum and a woodblock playing absolutely together

a note on a metallophone

three voices at once, on the same note

a guitar and a violin, plucking together, not the same note

43 The tape contains the following five timbres as examples:

1 Voice and trumpet on the same note.
2 Finger click and drum tap.
3 Low piano note.
4 Cymbal hit with hard stick, with hand holding the edge.
5 Trumpet and piano on the same note.

Choose the five timbres from your collection which you like best. Make a composition by putting them in the most effective order, perhaps using some more than once.

EXPLORING VOICE SOUNDS

In a way, this is about treating the voice as an instrument. The 20th-century composer who has probably done most to develop this aspect of the voice is the Italian, Luciano Berio. He has extended the possibilities of the voice so that they don't just include conventional singing. The voice is much wider than that, and can include such things as:

whispering

shouting

screaming

speaking, perhaps using different linguistic accents

squeaking

growling

There are many more possibilities. In order to hear them, listen to one or two of these compositions by Berio:

Circles

Sequenza III for female voice

Visage

Thema (*Omaggio a Joyce*)

The scores of the first two are well worth following, because of their methods of writing the music down and their use of visual imagination. The last two pieces, *Visage* and *Omaggio a Joyce*, both use the voice as an intriguing source of electronic sounds. You can learn more by also listening to:

Trevor Wishart: *Anticredos*

Ligeti: *Lux aeterna*

Both composers make adventurous use of the extended voice. Wishart in particular has made detailed study of what the voice and other parts of the body can achieve, including the use of lip buzzing, clapping, variation of the shape of the mouth, and many other techniques.

In our use of the voice, it is essential to have some understanding of the way other cultures use it. For instance, India, the Middle East, Africa and America can show a rich variety of techniques, which demonstrate that our idea of singing is only *one* way. In southern Africa they will whistle, croon, growl, whisper and include many other vocal sounds in their music. In American Indian singing you can hear slides and swoops, different kinds of shakes (vibratos), and nasal sounds. In Western music, you can also hear many styles of singing: compare blues with soul, opera with country and western, jazz scat with church choirs.

ASSIGNMENT 52 Produce and record as many different vocal timbres (tone colours) as possible. Here are a few suggestions:

whispering

singing

shouting

growling

throat vibration

singing and wobbling the chin

singing and rolling the tongue

screaming

sighing

speaking

VOICE HARMONICS

In Tibet, the Buddhist monks have developed unique ways of using their voices. Instead of concentrating just on a main note (the fundamental) produced by the voice, they have learnt to control the strength of the harmonics as well. At times, it seems that they are chanting several notes at once. It is difficult to explain how this is done, although it is to do with the main note being a very low one, around low C or B, and having a strong upper harmonic.

ASSIGNMENT 53 You can explore the harmonics of your own voice-sound by doing the following:

1 Choose an easily sung note.
2 On that note, pronounce EEOOEE, singing loudly.
3 Move very slowly and deliberately through the individual sounds of the word, changing the shape of your mouth as slowly as possible.
4 **Listen** very carefully. Part of this trick is learning to **hear** the harmonics: they are there all the time, but we don't normally notice them.

If you can use a microphone to help amplify and even record your voice, all the better.

After one or two tries, you will begin to hear the harmonic series changing above the note you are singing. If you do a very slow EE-OO, only gradually opening your mouth, you will hear the **descending** harmonic series; as you do OO-EE you will hear the **ascending** series.

An explanation of what is happening is that your mouth is actually moving through the complete series of vowel sounds, and each one of those sounds emphasises a different harmonic in the series.

Stockhausen's piece, *Stimmung*, the title of which literally means 'tuning', is based on the principle of the vocal control of harmonics. It is built from one chord:

44

with the six singers individually controlling the harmonics sounded above notes of the chord. On the tape you can hear the chord upon which *Stimmung* is based.

6 TEXTURE

You will recall from page 20 of this book that texture is to do with the particular 'feel' of a passage of music, and that the term originated from the weave patterns found in cloth. There are many different kinds of musical texture. Here we will explore some of them so that we can learn to make textures work for us.

HARMONY

Harmony is what happens when two or more notes are sounded at once. In the section on chords we learnt something about the handling of harmony – in itself a complex and fascinating area of music. But harmony can also be looked at from the point of view of texture.

For instance, you can have a simple harmony, or a complex one. A simple one might use just a few chords in a very straightforward manner, as in the harmonisation of this tune:

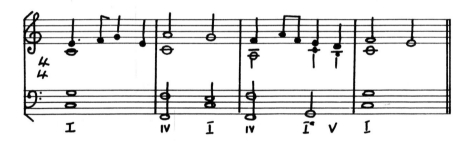

On the other hand, a complex passage might use many chords and lots of decorating notes as in this chorale harmonised by J. S. Bach:

'Laß, o Herr' harmonised by J. S. Bach

Another way of looking at harmonic textures is to describe them as being either planned, or created by 'inspired guesswork' (intuition). The harmony of much of our pop and jazz is created through this intuitive method.

ASSIGNMENT 54 A Form a group of four or five musicians. One should play the following tune on a suitable instrument:

Another should play a bass instrument, or the bass section of a keyboard.

Now experiment with adding bass and chords to the tune. Aim at 'feeling' for the right sounds through playing them – this is *not* a written assignment. Make several attempts, and when you are satisfied with one, record it. Take the time to listen to your final version, and perhaps sketch on paper some of the things you did.

B Using the same tune, try to create two other ways of adding harmony to it so that the texture is different. Listen to all three versions, listening for the contrasting harmonic textures.

One of the simplest and most effective ways of creating a harmonic texture from a tune is to use notes that move parallel with it. Medieval organum did this:

This music uses parallel fifths; similar effects can be found in the folk music of Iceland and Burma.

Stravinsky often used this technique with other intervals:

Of course, you don't have to use just parallel intervals: you can move whole chords up and down, 'shadowing' a melody. For example:

ASSIGNMENT 55

Treat the following tune in three ways:

1 Add one part to it, the interval of a fifth below.
2 Add one part, the interval of a second below.
3 Add two parts, each a third below the part above it.

Record all three versions, and then listen to them.

MAKING THE HARMONIC SERIES WORK FOR YOU

In the section on timbre, we learnt how to begin making interesting sounds and mixtures by using the harmonic series. It can also help us to create textures.

Look again at the way the pitches of the harmonic series are spaced:

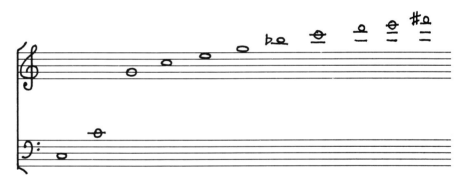

You can see that the higher we go up the series, the closer the intervals become. In our music, we can use this spacing in three different ways:

1 Notes very close together, like the top region of the harmonic series. For example:

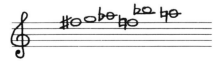

2 Notes spaced widely apart, like the bottom region of the series.

3 Using the whole of the spacing of the series.

These ideas about spacing can apply to whole sections of music, and not just to a chord. A piece might have a plan of textures which moved from type (1) to (2) to (3) and around them.

ASSIGNMENT 56 Make up a piece for any instrument or group of instruments. Use the following plan to decide the spacings of notes in the piece:

1st section	2nd	3rd	4th
notes well spaced	notes very close together	notes well spaced	a mixture of both

USING DRONES AND OSTINATOS TO CREATE TEXTURES

In the section on tunes, we discovered that drones and ostinatos can be very useful in creating the setting – the accompaniment – for a tune. They can also be used in their own right to create textures that are simple to construct but effective in their use.

Consider some of the possibilities suggested by the use of a drone:

1 A one-note drone. Against this, it is possible to do almost anything, using any notes and rhythms, and still make effective music. The drone acts as a kind of control, influencing and making sense of the rest of the music. On the tape, you can hear an example of this use of a drone. The notation can be shown as follows:

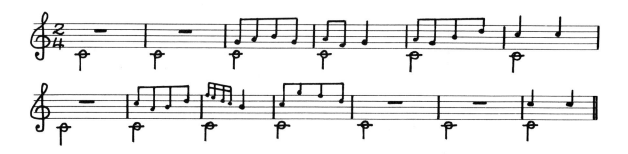

2 A two- or three-note drone. Otherwise as in (1) above.

 50

3 The drone moves from one set of sounds (instruments) to another, whilst other things are going on in the music.

 51

(notated in C)

4 The texture only consists of a series of overlapping drones or pedal-notes; tunes (or anything else) can later be superimposed on this texture, like objects in a landscape painting:

 52

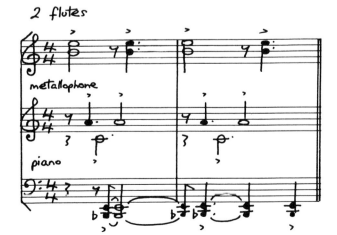

In some ways, the uses of ostinato are the same, although the music will sound more complex than with drones – less static. As an example, look at and listen to the use of the following ostinato idea:

Out of this idea we can create quite a complicated texture, by using it in a number of instruments:

🔲 53

As you can see and hear, some of the instruments vary the ostinato pattern.

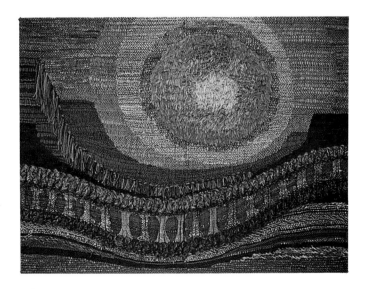

Handwoven tapestry, 'Red Centre' by the Australian artist, Ben Shearer

78

A second approach to ostinato is to use a number of different ones at once. This can create an exciting texture through a simple method:

Notice the number of patterns used at once, their individual length, and the speed at which they are played when compared with each other. All these things help to shape the music, creating

◆ EXCITEMENT (tension)

or

◆ CALM (lack of tension)

as the composer sees fit.

ASSIGNMENT 57

1 Form a small group of musicians.
2 Each invents an ostinato pattern which is played to the others.
3 Devise three different ways of fitting the patterns together. For example, everybody enters one by one, everybody plays together for a while, then people drop out one by one; or work out a more sophisticated scheme than this.
4 Record and compare your three versions.

SEVERAL TUNES AT ONCE

It is possible to create exciting and interesting textures by having a number of different tunes at once. Listen to the following examples of this texture:

Tippett: Concerto for Double String Orchestra, third movement

Ives: 'The Housatonic at Stockbridge' from *Three Places in New England*

Britten: 'Tema Seriale con Fuga' Part 2, No. VIII from *Cantata academica, carmen basiliense*

There are a number of ways of approaching many-tuned, or polyphonic textures:

1 One is to have much the same tune in each part, with some anticipation and decoration. This technique is often called **heterophony**, meaning that everybody is performing – at the same time – different versions of the same tune. Study the following example, which is also on the tape:

Keyboards

2 As we discovered earlier (page 79), we can use a number of ostinatos at once to create a polyphonic texture.
3 We can make a drone texture, as described on pages 76 and 77, then compose or improvise tunes out of the drone notes.
4 We can make up a sequence of chords – for example:

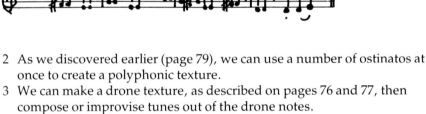

and then compose several melodic lines using the notes of the chords, in the correct order, as a framework:

5 We can simply combine totally unrelated tunes in a kind of glorious 'jam' session, as in Ives's piece, *The Fourth of July*, or in free jazz.

ASSIGNMENT 58 Choose two of the methods of combining tunes described on pages 80 and 81. Improvise a version of one of them; compose and perform a version of the other. Make both fairly short 'bursts' of music, say about 30 seconds long.

Finally, two ideas about what you might do with all these textures you have created:

1 Combine them, simply by piling them on top of each other. You will either need a fair-sized group of musicians (the school/college band or orchestra) or you could use a multi-track tape-recorder.
2 Alternate different types of texture. Stravinsky's *The Rite of Spring* can be studied from this point of view. The changes of texture vary from the abrupt to the smooth; textures may be used for a long or short time. Listen to:

Part 1: 'The Adoration of The Earth' – Introduction
Part 2: 'The Sacrifice' – Sacrificial Dance

ASSIGNMENT 59 Compose a short 'experimental' version of (1) and (2) above, for the school/college orchestra or band. The notation need not be complex and detailed, because it is the interplay of types of texture that is most important here, and textures easily lend themselves to an approximate, graphic kind of notation. Here is an example to help you:

(a) collage

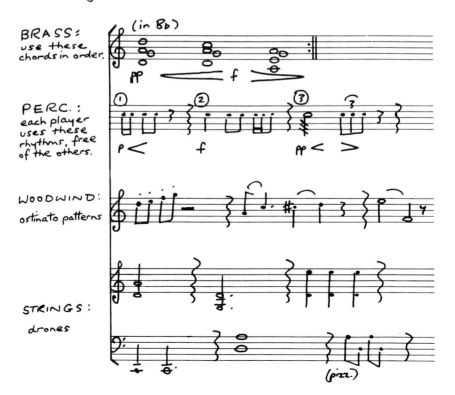

(b) alternating textures

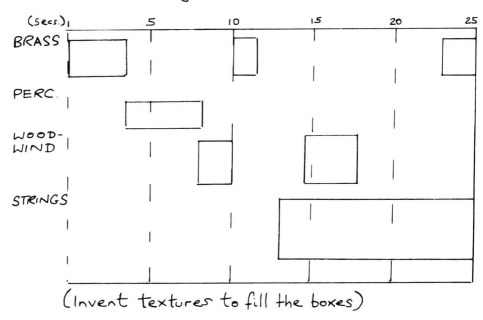

(Invent textures to fill the boxes)

7 STRUCTURING

Although in our explorations of composing we may not be concerned to make pieces which are longer than one or two minutes, it would be a mistake to say that we can therefore ignore structuring as a dimension of music. In the world's art, there are plenty of examples of shorter things containing intricate structure; for instance, Japanese haiku poetry, and the music of Webern (for example, the Concerto, Opus 24, for 9 instruments). As a way of thinking (imagining), structuring is important and can be exciting.

Examine the visual shapes on the opposite page.

The visual can provide us with a number of clues about the way structuring works in music. The world is full of interesting visual shapes, each of which has its own particular structure. Consider the following:

PYRAMIDS

CHAIRS

HOUSES

BRIDGES

Each *must* have a structure which works, and doesn't just *look* good, for obvious reasons! One of these examples, houses, can be useful to us in considering one of the two main dimensions of musical structuring. David Reck, in *Music of the Whole Earth* (page 403), quotes a child who said:

◆ MUSIC IS THE HOUSE THAT SOUNDS LIVE IN

This is an excellent way of expressing the relationship between the sounds and the structure of music: they are inseparable. You could even go so far as to say music *is* structured sound. Structuring is a combination of

◆ musical architecture

and

◆ musical drama or psychology

Here are some of the considerations which help to make musical structure.

BEGINNINGS AND ENDINGS

In a way, these can act like the outer walls, or even the entrance and exit of the building. Beginnings and endings can colour a whole piece. For instance, you can have a sudden beginning, and a fade-out kind of ending. You can even have a special introductory section, before the piece gets properly under way.

Form a group of any number of musicians.

A Improvise versions of each of the following types of beginning:

   sudden

   gradually getting going

   start with an accompaniment pattern – add a tune (or tunes) on top

   an introduction, ending with a short hint of the main section

B Improvise versions of each of the following types of ending. Obviously, you will have to imagine what goes before in the music – you can then make up the music which comes just before the ending.

   stop abruptly

   the music collapses

   gradually wind down, and slow down

   one instrument settles on a long note, signalling the end

   a fade-out ending

   a special closing section, called a coda

USING LANGUAGE TO HELP STRUCTURE MUSIC

Language can be a splendid source of ideas about the structuring of music. In exploring tunes, we came across the idea of phrases forming sequences of questioning and answering. This in itself is an effective approach to structuring music. We can have:

   ◆ musical conversations

   ◆ an incomplete musical idea in one instrument/voice completed by another

Words in themselves can be material for a composer. They contain a wealth of implied sounds and can also generate structure, in the sense that one word can contain the structural design for a complete work. As an example, take the word

   REVENGE

This is a word with two syllables. Of the two, the second one is accented, with the first one leading up to it. We might therefore use this word as a metaphor for a piece in two main sections, in the same relationship to each other as the syllables in the word – that is, section 2 is more important than section 1. (You might like to think about the musical devices which would help to make the relationship clear. For instance, section 1 begins quietly, with a gradual *crescendo* to the beginning of section 2, which is loud.) With the word 'revenge', we should also think about the end of the word, the 'ge' part of it. What sort of ending would this imply for a piece of music? Perhaps a very abrupt cut-off, rather than a fade-out.

Before leaving this example, consider the actual sounds contained in the word. The 're' sound implies a gradual opening out. You might have percussion, say a snare drum doing a roll, for the equivalent of the 'r' sound, and a chord using several pitched instruments for the more open, pitched, sound of the 'e'.

ASSIGNMENT 61

Choose one of the following words. Use it to create the **structure** of a piece, remaining as true as possible to everything implied by the word. Of course, actual choice of instruments and voices should result from the chosen word.

DARKNESS   TRIPS

ACTIVITY   CONSTELLATION

WORLD

STRUCTURAL PRINCIPLES

You will already be familiar with some of these, but they are worth re-instating, in the context of an assignment.

ASSIGNMENT 62 **A**

Repetition
Invent a musical idea on an instrument. Make a short section of music out of it; repeat that section. (This is rather like playing 'pass the parcel', except that you are *adding* wrappers, not taking them off.)

B

Varied repetition
Make up a short section of music for any instrument or voice. Record it and write it down. Make a varied version of the same section. Play/sing them one after the other.

C

Contrast
Make up a short section of music as before. Study closely what you did in it. Follow it with another section which contrasts with it: if the first section was slow, make the second fast; if the first was quiet, make the second loud; and so on.

On the tape, there are versions of all three of the above. Here is the written notation of them:

87

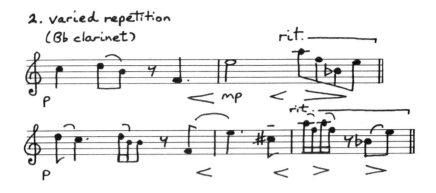

2. varied repetition
(Bb clarinet)

3. contrast
(flute)

ASSIGNMENT 63

Here are some ways of expressing contrast – opposition – in words:

simple music/complicated music

relaxed music/tense music

familiar music/new music

See if you can improvise music for each.

USING ENVELOPE TO CREATE STRUCTURE

As we discovered in the section on timbre, **envelope** is a way of describing the three elements which make up a sound:

- ◆ ATTACK
- ◆ SUSTAIN
- ◆ RELEASE

If we use these elements to help our thinking with regard to structure, they can be extremely useful. Instead of just representing parts of one sound, they can become whole sections of a piece, as follows:

◆ INTRODUCTION

◆ MIDDLE (MAIN) SECTION

◆ ENDING (CODA)

1 Study some of the pieces of music listed below, seeing (hearing!) if you can identify these three elements in the structure. If you wish, you can use the references given here when following with a score.

Beethoven	Piano Sonata in F#, Op. 78, first movement	
	introduction	bars 1 to 4
	main section	bars 5 to 94
	coda	bar 95 to end
Copland	Suite from the ballet *Appalachian Spring*	
	(This piece has an introduction, then six sections, then a coda.)	
Stravinsky	Symphony in C, first movement	
	introduction	figures 1 to 5
	main section	figures 5 to 71
	coda	figure 71 to end
Schubert	'Gute Nacht' from *Winterreise*, Op. 89	

2 Compose a piece of your own, using this envelope idea to provide your structure. A version of this is on the tape.

 60

FINAL PROJECT

THE GREAT AMBUSH

The Great Ambush is a famous piece for the p'i-p'a, a type of Chinese lute. It dates from about AD 580, and its Chinese name looks like this:

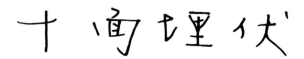

61
On the tape you can hear the complete piece (11 minutes), performed by Wong Ching-Ping. The make-up of its sections is important. They form a kind of programme, depicting a battle between the armies of the Han people, commanded by Liu-Baun, and of the Chu people, under Shiang-Yu. Here are the titles of the sections:

1 The gathering of the troops
2 The troops line up
3 Drum beats
4 Bugle calls
5 Artillery barrage
6 The troops form up
7 The armies march
8 The ambush
9 The skirmish
10 The Chu soldiers are frightened
11 Artillery fire
12 The battle
13 Shouts of battle
14 The charge
15 The siege
16 The call to retreat
17 Death of the Chu general
18 The triumph of the Han army

Listen to the whole piece. Then listen again, and try to identify the sections as you listen to the tape. You will notice the use of some simple devices to convey the character of the music. In sections 5 and 11 you can even hear imitation of the guns firing, and in sections 9 and 12 you can hear some of the sounds of battle.

After you have listened to the whole piece, concentrate on the following sections, which are identified for you on the tape.

1 The gathering of the troops
3 Drum beats
5 Artillery barrage
12 The battle
17 Death of the Chu general

It is your task to compose your own version of these sections, for any available combination of instruments and/or voices. To help you, here are some suggestions for each of the sections:

Section 1 could be a tune.

Section 3 could explore rhythm and metre.

Section 5 could explore timbre.

Section 12 could make adventurous use of words and word-sounds.

Section 17 could mainly use chords.

Once you have composed and rehearsed all these sections, you can perform a short version of *The Great Ambush*, by playing the sections you have composed.

As a final exercise, you should tape-record your sections, and listen to the result.

It is interesting to note that Wong Ching-Ping's performance of this piece is his own version, and therefore unique. You have now helped to make another version as part of your response to the p'i-p'a music. This is exactly what composing is about, and although the title of this book is *Learning to Compose*, in some ways it could easily have been called *Composing to Learn*. I hope you enjoy your further explorations in composing.

A COMPOSER'S RESOURCE BANK

The following is a summing-up of helpful procedures contained in the book. Refer to this section as an aid to your composing, and as a kind of checklist to assist your thinking and your musical imagination.

WAYS OF BEGINNING
1 A sudden beginning
2 Gradually getting going
3 Start with an accompaniment pattern, add the tune afterwards
4 A special introductory section

WAYS OF ENDING
1 Stop suddenly
2 Make the music 'collapse'
3 Gradually wind the music down, slowing the tempo
4 One instrument/voice settles on a long note, signalling the end
5 A fade-out ending
6 A special closing section, called a coda

STRUCTURES/ SHAPES
Some possibilities
1 In sections
2 Continuous music
3 Building up to a climax

WAYS OF CONTINUING
1 Variation
2 Repetition
3 Contrast

CONTOURS
1 Constant repetition of one note
2 Adding notes on either side of a single note
3 Using a wave shape
4 Using a falling shape
5 Using an arch shape
6 Using an upward shape

TUNE-MAKING
You can make a tune from
1 a scale of any type
2 a chord or set of chords
3 by making notes follow an imaginary (or a drawn) line
4 by using unpredictability
5 by mixing steps and leaps
6 by filling in the spaces between long notes

TUNE-SETTING	1 Adding a drone
	2 Adding an ostinato
	3 Adding chords
	4 Using one instrument to play an introduction, an ending, and a simple accompaniment line

ORNAMENTS	1 Grace notes, singly or in groups
	2 Leaning notes (appoggiaturas)
	3 Turning shapes
	4 Repeated notes
	5 Sliding and slurring between notes
	6 Trills

TEXTURES	1 A tune with simple harmony
	2 A tune with complicated harmony
	3 A tune plus parallel fifths (or other interval)
	4 Using the upper region of the harmonic series
	5 Using the lower region of the harmonic series
	6 Using the whole spacing of the harmonic series
	7 Drone/ostinato textures
	8 Several tunes at once (polyphony, counterpoint)
	9 Everybody has a different version of the *same* tune (heterophony)

CHORD TYPES	1 Triads (I, IV and V)
	2 Using one interval (for example, the second)
	3 Using many types of interval
	4 Built out of a region of the harmonic series

USING TIMBRE	Using timbre means using
	1 harmonics in different combinations
	2 envelope: attack, sustain, release
	3 resonance: the shape of the 'body' making the sound, and the material from which it is made

FINALLY

◆ COMPOSING IS MAKING SOMETHING WITH SOUNDS

LISTENING LIST

GETTING STARTED

Gamelan	Balinese gamelan music (*WOMAD Talking Book*, Vol. 1, side 1 band 3)
	Javanese Court Gamelan, Vol. 2 (Nonesuch, H-72074)
Heterophony	'Hua San Liu', from *Popular Jiangnan Music* (Hong Kong Records, 4.340094 (cassette))
Messiaen	*Catalogue d'oiseaux*, any book
Schoenberg	No. 2 of *Sechs kleine Klavierstücke*, Op. 19

1 TIME

Bartók	'Six Dances in Bulgarian Rhythm', *Mikrokosmos*, Bk VI
	Concerto for Orchestra, 1st movement
Bernstein	'America', from *West Side Story*
Birtwistle	*Chronometer*
Davies	*Antechrist*
Debussy	'Jeux de Vagues', from *La Mer*
Gamelan	See 'Getting started' above
Haydn	Symphony No. 100 ('The Military'), last movement
Indian music	Ragas, *Songs of India* (Folkways, FG 3530)
Ives	'Putnam's Camp, Redding, Connecticut', from *Three Places in New England*
	The Fourth of July
Japanese music	*Japanese Treasures with Shamisen and Shakuhachi* (Lyrichord, LLST 7228)
Messiaen	*Et exspecto resurrectionem mortuorum*, 1st and 2nd movements
	Catalogue d'oiseaux
Schoenberg	No. 2 of *Sechs kleine Klavierstücke*, Op. 19
Stravinsky	*Petrushka*, First Tableau
	The Rite of Spring:
	Part 1: 'The Adoration of the Earth' – Introduction
	Part 2: 'The Sacrifice' – Sacrificial Dance
	Symphonies of Wind Instruments

2 TUNE

African music	*Africa: South of the Sahara* (Folkways, FE 4503)
	a wave-shaped contour: Bulu song, band 28
	a falling contour: Twa song, band 14
Bach	Fugue in C minor, from *48 Preludes and Fugues*, Book 1
Bagpipe music	*Northumbrian Folk* (BBC Records, REC 118S)
	'Rakish Paddy' (*WOMAD Talking Book*, Vol. 1, side 2 band 5)

NOTE: *Folkways recordings may be obtained through Stern's, 116 Whitfield Street, London W1P 5RW, telephone 01-387 5550.*

Bartók	'Boating' from *Mikrokosmos* Bk V
Beethoven	Piano Sonata in G, Op. 79, 1st movement
Berio	*Folk Songs*, Songs 1 and 2
Chant	*Medieval Music: Sacred Monophony*, The Oxford Anthology of Music (OUP 161)
Chinese music	*China's Instrumental Heritage* (Lyrichord, LLST 792)
	Chinese Classical Music (Lyrichord, LL 72)
	The Chinese Cheng (Lyrichord, LLST 7302)
Handel	Courante from Suite in G
Indian music	Ragas, *Songs of India* (Folkways, FG 3530)
Medieval organum	*Early Medieval Music up to 1300,* side 3 band 5, The History of Music in Sound, Vol. 2 (EMI, HLP 4)
Messiaen	*Quartet for the End of Time*, III Abîme des oiseaux
Miles Davis	*Tallest Trees* (Prestige, 24012)
Mingus	*Mariachis* (*The Street Musicians*) (RCA PL 10939)
Mozart	Clarinet Quintet, 2nd movement
	Piano Sonata in F, K332, 1st movement
	Piano Sonata in C, K545, 1st movement

3 WORDS

Berio	*Sinfonia*, 2nd and 3rd movements
Britten	'Nocturne' and 'Hymn' from *Serenade* for tenor, horn and strings
Ives	Songs: 'The Circus Band' and 'Charlie Rutledge'
Marley	'Chant down Babylon' and 'Buffalo Soldier', on *Confrontation* (Island Records, 1983)
Schubert	*Erlkönig*
Tippett	Opening Chorus from *A Child of Our Time*
Weelkes	Madrigals: 'As Vesta was from Latmos Hill descending' and 'O Care, thou wilt despatch me'

4 CHORDS

Blues	*Muddy Waters at Newport* (1960) (Green Line Records, GCH-8022)
	T-Bone Walker: The Collection (Déjà Vu, DVLP 2047)
Lutosławski	Symphony No. 3 (particularly opening sections)
Schoenberg	No. 2 of *Sechs kleine Klavierstücke*, Op. 19

5 TIMBRE

African music	*Africa: South of the Sahara* (Folkways, FE 4503) Use of the voice: Swazi Song, band 2 Bushman songs, bands 5 and 6
Berio	*Sequenza III* for female voice
	Visage
	Thema (*Omaggio a Joyce*)
Britten	'Prelude' and 'Postlude' from Serenade for tenor, horn and strings
Cage	*Sonatas and Interludes* (for prepared piano)

Crumb	*Ancient Voices of Children*, Section IV
Ives	'The Housatonic at Stockbridge', from *Three Places in New England*, beginning to Ⓓ
Jazz (scat singing)	Louis Armstrong, 'Skid-dat-de-dat' on *The Louis Armstrong Legend* (World Records, P42; 4-record set)
Ligeti	*Aventures, Nouvelles Aventures, Lux aeterna*
Messiaen	*Et exspecto resurrectionem mortuorum*, 3rd movement
Stockhausen	*Stimmung*
Tibetan music	*Tibet: Musique rituelle* (Radio France, OCR49 MM57) *Ancient and Oriental Music*, The History of Music in Sound, Vol. 1 (EMI, HLP1)
Varèse	*Ionisation*
Webern	Five Pieces for Orchestra, Op. 10, 1st and 2nd pieces
Wishart	*Anticredos* (available from the composer, Trevor Wishart, c/o Music Dept, Keele University, Staffs.)

6 TEXTURE

Bach	Fugue in C minor, from *48 Preludes and Fugues*, Book 1 Chorales: 'Laß, o Herr, dein Ohr sich neigen' 'Jesu, meine Freude' *St Matthew Passion* (the chorale settings)
Britten	'Tema Seriale con Fuga', Part 2 No. VIII of *Cantata Academica, Carmen Basiliense*
Crumb	*Ancient Voices of Children*, Section V
Heterophony	'Hua San Liu', from *Popular Jiangnan Music* (Hong Kong Records, 4.340094 (cassette))
Ives	'Putnam's Camp, Redding, Connecticut', from *Three Places in New England*, beginning to Ⓔ
Ravel	*Boléro*
Stravinsky	*Petrushka*, First Tableau, beginning to ⑳
Tippett	Concerto for Double String Orchestra, 3rd movement
Webern	Concerto, Op. 24, for nine instruments, 2nd movement Five Pieces for Orchestra, Op. 10, 3rd piece

7 STRUCTURING

Beethoven	Symphony No. 5 in C minor Piano Sonata in F sharp, Op. 7
Berio	*Sinfonia*, 2nd and 3rd movements
Copland	Suite from the ballet *Appalachian Spring*
Lutosławski	*Jeux Vénitiens* *Chain I*
Schubert	'Gute Nacht', from *Winterreise*, Op. 89
Stravinsky	Symphony in C, 1st movement Symphonies of Wind Instruments
Varèse	*Intégrales*